Secrets Men Don't Want Women To Know

Will Willis Jr.

Published by Willis & Associates LLC, 205 Coconut Key Drive, Palm Beach Gardens, Florida 33418
Email: WWillis007@aol.com

Printed in the United States of America

Design by Phyllis Chotin, Chotin Communications, Inc.
Email: pchotin@chotincommunications.com

ISBN 0-9670832-1-4

I dedicate this book to all of the wonderful women in my life.

Although there are far too many to name them all, some are of particular importance to me. To my mother, thank you for bringing me into this world. It was, I'm sure, no small feat given that there were two of us. To my twin sister, I can only say thank God we don't have to dress alike any longer. To my three daughters, Kimberly, Kelly, and Katie, thank you for providing me with the first hand validation that women are in fact the stronger sex. To Phyllis, thank you for being a wonderful partner and for providing me with the expertise needed to make this book concept become a reality. Toni, thanks for giving me access to your women's mentoring group and for providing me with the motivation to write this book. And to Jean and Alexis, the two loves of my life who provide me with the daily motivation and inspiration to make them the happiest women in the world.

TABLE OF CONTENTS

INTRODUCTION

I was not a bad person. Nor was I a bad father. What I was, was a bad husband. A very bad husband — a terrible husband, in fact, though the truth of that escaped me for a long time. By then I'd botched two marriages and came to the conclusion that George Bernard Shaw was absolutely right when he observed that youth is wasted on the young.

Believe me, not a day goes by that I don't think about the damage I did, both to my ex-wives and to my children, by my neglect and, yes, my indiscretions. Which is why I decided to write this book. Not only did I want to make peace with my past, but also to pass on the wisdom I've reluctantly achieved in my middle age — wisdom gained by learning from my mistakes. That's the problem with wisdom; it usually comes from making mistakes. I can honestly say I have earned every one of the gray hairs on my head!

But the truth is that these mistakes don't necessarily have

to be your own. Smart people can learn from others' mistakes and in that way avoid making the same ones themselves. That's my hope — that by reading this book you'll be able to prove Shaw wrong. If my advice and insights can keep even one person from turning down a wrong path, I'll consider this book an overwhelming success.

A few months before I began writing, when I was still jotting down notes and memories and creating an outline, I told a good friend what I planned to do. We were eating lunch at the time, and I remember him almost choking on his steak before breaking into hysterical laughter. "You?" he said between gasps. "You?! Writing a book for women?" Hahahaha.

I was ready for him, though. I'd just recently seen the Leonardo DiCaprio movie "Catch Me If You Can," about a forger and con man who stole several million dollars before getting busted by the FBI. It's based on a true story, and according to an on-screen note before the end credits, the guy is now paid many millions a year to advise banks and large companies how to avoid, yes, forgers and con men just like him. Who better to spot sinners than a sinner?

Checkmate. Security companies hire convicted burglars to help them develop security systems. Software companies hire hackers to help them make their software hack-proof. And you, in a sense, can hire me, an admitted "Bad Boy", to help you with your marriage or primary relationship.

Despite my admittedly checkered past with relationships, I have always, believe it or not, been a passionate supporter of women — and I don't mean just divorce settlements and child-support payments. I mean that my four daughters, two sisters, two ex-wives, sister-in-law, and three former sisters-in-law (in addition to numerous female business associates and friends) are just a few of the millions of women whom I'd like the world to treat much better than it seems to. Despite decades of truly excellent progress, in many ways women are still discriminated against. While it's wonderful to see them move from the kitchen to the office and break down the walls to the ol' boys' CEO club — like Carly Fiorina, chairman of Hewlett-Packard — when it comes to marriage and divorce, women are still viewed as the weaker sex and are often treated as second-class citizens. This is less about discrimination, I think, than about discriminating taste. In my experience, women frequently get poor legal advice and end up with the thorns instead of the roses when it comes to divorce negotiations and settlements.

My objective here is to empower women by revealing secrets that men may not even know they're keeping, and in that way increase the odds that their marriages will succeed. Personally, I'd like to turn the current marriage-divorce ratio on its head and see divorce become as rare as 70-year marriages are now. And for that I've got a lot of strategies, as you'll soon read. One of them involves giving women tips to avoid marriages that are doomed before they say, "I do." Others offer techniques for saving that, which can be saved.

It's true, though, that some marriages are already beyond repair. In those cases, what I can provide is solid advice for keeping women from pulling a Clara Harris — that is, reacting to the pain and frustration of divorce by doing something that makes the Three Stooges read like Jane Austen. Harris, you'll recall, is the middle-aged Houston woman who ran over her husband three times with her Mercedes in a hotel parking lot after seeing him in the lobby with his young lover. It goes without saying, I think, that she'd probably like to rethink that reaction now. While divorce can and does make people irrational, no man is worth the price of spending the rest of your life pressing Texas license plates and sharing a bunk with a butch named Ginger.

At this point, the greatest assurance I can give you that what you're about to read really works, I give you…me! I have been in a completely fabulous, supportive, perfect, mutually satisfying relationship for years now, which is to say that pigs can indeed fly if you give them strong enough wings. And you **can** teach old dogs new tricks.

What's that you say, that the third time's the charm? That I've grown up and am better myself, and that's why my relationship works? Au contraire. The only factor that's changed this time around is that my partner has been empowered by what I'm about to reveal to you; what I've revealed to her has allowed her to take control of our relationship.

From the bottom of my heart, I've never been happier. I can even accept that this sort of happiness was actually available to me both the first and second times around, if only I'd been wise enough. That I have it now is enough — or it will be when I share it with you.

Chapter 1

HAPPY WIFE, HAPPY LIFE

A friend once asked me to come by and help him move his last remaining things out of the house he had to sell after his divorce. The movers had done a pretty good job. All that was left were a few stray CD's and a chest of drawers he'd kept in the garage for his tools. After we got everything loaded in his station wagon, we stood in the doorway where he'd spent eight good years and two not-so-good years, and scanned to make sure nothing had been left behind. "Well, I guess that's it," he said, fighting tears.

"Wait," I said, spotting a five by five frame hanging on a nail in the corner. Not till I got close did I see that it was a blue needlepoint of words on a beige background: "If mama ain't happy," it said, "ain't no one happy."

I handed it to him.

6

"Damn right," he muttered (actually that's the cleaned-up version), flinging it into the bushes for the new owner to discover someday during brush clearance.

If mama ain't happy, ain't no one happy. Some men, like my friend, accept the unerring wisdom of those eight little words far too late. Strictly speaking, you can substitute wife for mama here, because even in a home without children present, if the woman's not happy, the man won't be either. Conversely, if she is, so will he be. Which means, of course, that the wise man does what he can to make his wife happy.

So why am I telling you, a woman, about this? Because it's critical that women realize how they control the happiness quotient in their families and relationships. Women, in fact, are the ones who have most of the real power in relationships. How they use, or don't use, that power determines the amount of happiness they, and their partners, will achieve.

Back to that in a moment, right after some pertinent facts about me: One, I'd owned a white Jaguar automobile for more than half my adult life. Sure, I'd bought newer cars every few years, but always a Jaguar and always in white; never an SUV or sports car, and never ever that quintessential yuppie exclamation point, a BMW. Two, I've always refused to date women who already had children, becuase I didn't want to get involved with anyone else's baggage, having enought of my own —but, if they were going to have a child, I told myself, it would have to be a boy, since I didn't have any sons of my own. And three, I never liked pets in my home; too much of a neat freak!

So why am I telling you all of this? Because about seven years ago I fell in love with a woman who had a four-year-old daughter. And now my hard and fast rules that took over fifty years to develop were overnight rendered soft and slow. Here came this woman whose happiness became my most important priority. So not only do I have a beautiful blonde stepdaughter, but right at this moment, peeing on my carpet and shedding on the couch are two yellow Labradors; meanwhile, the car I see parked in my driveway is a black SUV made by BMW!

The point?

Women rule.

If only they understood that better, men wouldn't stand a chance — and it would be for the good of both.

In truth, the woman who doesn't flex her feminine muscles and choose to rule is either not trying or doesn't have the right man. Whichever one is true, it's up to her to recognize the situation, admit the truth, and work to control it. A man who loves his woman absolutely will do whatever he can to make her happy, even if it entails going against his own personal desires. Ultimately, he has to come to realize that the attainment of his own personal desires and, indeed, happiness depends on his giving her what she needs to be happy first.

I've known for a long time that women have the ability to control men, and that they are, without question, not the weaker sex. In fact, women generally handle most stressful situations better than men. Take pain, for example. God was wise in giving child-birth and menstruation to women. If these functions were in men's domain, the human race would've reached extinction long before even Moses. Go ahead, ask the lab technician the next time you have to have blood taken which sex handles the needle better. Invariably, they'll tell you it's women, and regale you with stories of big football players who have to lie down so they don't faint at the sight of a needle.

Then, too, women are strong enough to conciliate. Instead of having to win outright all the time, the way men tend to; they're strong enough to try to create win-win situations for all.

And therein lies most of the problem: Women often don't understand the power that they have, or don't know how to use it, because they've spent millennia trying to spread it around.

The truth is that men are rather easily managed, motivated, and manipulated. Essentially, all you have to do is satisfy their basic hungers for food and sex. If you do (and food is strictly optional), then you can get just about anything you want and need.

I know it sounds primitive, but hey, even differential calculus is built on simple arithmetic. The most complicated of men is still driven by the same primitive desires, and the younger the man, the truer this is. Young men think about sex — how, where, and with whom — about once every six seconds, which seems like a lot until you consider that old men think about it about every 18 seconds. By then they've learned to control themselves a bit, and they've also, after a divorce or two, realized that a relationship's sexual component is less important than the friendship, mutual trust, and respect it's built on. After all, such are the basis of great sex (along with jewelry and furs).

I recently went to a wild bachelor party. Suffice it to say that this was the bachelor's party bachelor's party, with naked women running around and drunken men chasing wantonly after them. Once upon a time I myself would've been one of these guys, but thanks to my wonderful mate, who's trained me not to think with my dick, I hung back and just watched. How, I wondered, would I feel if she did the same thing at a bachelorette party? I'd feel awful, came the answer. Now, I know that sounds like the most obvious realization, but it wasn't the kind of thing I'd ever before considered — or rather, that my manhood considered. Thanks to my partner, who literally trained me to consider that the knife cuts both ways, I'm now able to understand the joke about a man who comes home flat drunk at three in the morning, pounding at the door to wake his wife because he's forgotten his keys — and thinking he's in big trouble. But when he wakes with a miserable hangover several hours later, he finds himself in bed and wearing pajamas. In comes his smiling wife, bringing him hot coffee and breakfast. He asks about the loving treatment, which he doesn't think he deserves, considering the hour he'd come home and the condition he was in. "Well," she says, "when I tried to take off your clothes and get you into bed, you said, 'Forget it, lady, I'm married.'"

I promise, I wouldn't have understood that joke before my partner helped me to understand the necessity of thinking through the consequences of my actions. Since she did, I've come to realize that a few minutes of pleasure is not worth jeopardizing our long-term relationship. And oddly enough, I find the restriction absolutely liberating.

The bottom line is that you as a woman have the ability to control your own happiness. Whether or not you can control the situation you find yourself in, you can at least control your reaction to it. As Eleanor Roosevelt said, "No one can make you feel inferior without your consent." Or, in the words of a motivational speaker I once heard, "If you can't change the situation, change your attitude."

In truth, people can't and won't make you angry or happy or sad or anything. Only you can do that. If you think you're miserable, you'll probably be miserable. If you think you can't get a date because you have children, you probably won't. If you think life has dealt you a losing hand, you've already lost.

I understand, of course, how natural it is to feel bitter or negative about men after you come out of a bad relationship. It's difficult, if not impossible, to hide your negative feelings. But if left unchecked, this negativism can continue to grow and take over your whole life. And soon enough you'll view the whole world through that bleak prism, which becomes like a magnet and attracts more bleakness your way, which of course carries on the cycle indefinitely.

An alternative is to grieve for a while and then move on. Look back at the years of your relationship as an opportunity to learn and grow. If you've paid for the lesson, you may as well learn from it; better you should take the learning and move forward with the attitude that you won't make the same mistakes again. That's called growth.

You *weren't* meant to go through life alone. And you *were* meant to find someone special. Never forget that. It will help you make it through the darkest times.

Chapter 2

REASONS WHY COUPLES STAY TOGETHER

Some people are so terrified of divorce that they never marry. Don't laugh. It's true. Not marrying is the only guaranteed way to avoid divorce — just like not crossing the street is the only way to avoid getting hit by a car, and not flying is the only way to avoid plane crashes. For the fearful, not doing is the way to avoid failing. Similarly, there are countless marriages kept together by either fear of (admitting) failure or fear of the unknown (being single).

Over the years I've heard five-dozen reasons why some people stay with cruel, moronic, even satanic spouses who have demonstrated time and again that they will never change their ways. But even the best and most compelling reasons are, to me, no better than excuses.

Maybe I'm shaped by my childhood. I will always remember the way my parents fought. I'd sit on the front steps crying while they shouted at each other — and then ran out to ask me which of them was in the right. They callously tried to make me their judge and jury — me, a nine-year-old. And yet they continued to stay together "for the sake of the kids." Obviously, their staying together was nobly intended, but just as obviously it was a terrible idea, one built along the road to hell. The hostile environment their bad feelings created was much harder on my siblings and me than their divorce could possibly have been.

For good reasons, I think, this subject fascinates me. So over the years, through research and conversations with divorced friends and acquaintances, I've managed to identify the six most common reasons why couples remain together long after they both know that the marriage has flat-lined:

1. For the good of the kids.

As reasons go, this is probably the best of them. Sociologists, psychologists, educators, and anyone with common sense can tell you that kids stand the best chance in this world when two loving parents raise them. They do better in school, have fewer run-ins with the law, and are more likely to lead healthy, productive lives as adults. So it makes sense to try and stick it out "for the good of the kids." Unfortunately, the operative phrase here is "two loving parents." If the parents are too busy hating each other, they can't possibly be loving the kids. In reality, two hostile parents in the home are probably going to do more damage to the kids' psyches than two calm single parents. Take me, for example. My parents stayed together at least six years longer than they should have, and all that time I internalized their arguing and crying and tension. To what good?

2. Money.

From what I've seen, it seems that troubled couples with at least some amount of money to their names tend to stay together longer, fearing the economic repercussions. Those with absolutely no money feel like they have nothing to lose, so they'll quickly split up. Then, too, men are generally more likely to try to tough out a tough marriage, hoping to avoid financial consequences that would undermine their "self worth", which is of course intimately linked to their "net worth". They lose their minds at the thought of losing half of what they've made, and they wonder fearfully whether they'll ever get back what they've lost. I can speak from personal experience on that too. I stayed in my second marriage long after it was legally and ethically dead, because I couldn't stand the thought of losing what I'd worked so hard to accumulate. Not until I suffered a few bad business deals and was nearly broke anyway did I realize I had nothing left to lose. Some women, in my experience, tend to be somewhat less materialistic than men, more focused on the quality of their personal lives and family lives, and less tied to the ego issues that money can raise. Additionally, women tend to be more optimistic about their chances at happiness following a divorce, thinking that they'll cash out after the settlement.

3. Business.

A corollary of the money reason is the business reason. In tough economic times, there are inevitable layoffs. In turn, layoffs lead to people being forced to start their own businesses, often with their spouses as partners and life savings as their only capital. Well, here again, common sense tells you that a couple fighting for their economic lives is facing a fair amount of stress, particularly if they work together 24/7. Into that equation, factor in the stresses of an already bad marriage. What you get then is a hideous marriage that can't be dissolved for fear of being up the proverbial river without a paddle. Meanwhile, the situation for a battling couple who owns a *successful* business is only somewhat different. That yields a man who doesn't want to liquidate or sell out in order to settle a divorce dispute — a man exactly like a friend of mine. He had an exceptionally successful business but was miserable in his marriage; he actually hated his wife, who happened to be his partner. Getting out of the marriage would've meant getting out of the business, which he wasn't willing to do. So, still counting wedding anniversaries (30, to date), he settles for girlfriends on the side — more of them, I suspect, than anyone but Hugh Hefner. His wife isn't blind to his philandering, but she doesn't use all the leverage she has;

with the aid of even a competent attorney, she could extricate herself from what is, at best, a sad relationship, and walk away with a pile of dough. Instead, she buys into her husband's psychological war games. What he does every now and then, when she starts making noises, is guilt-trip her into believing that she's the one who's "destroying everything" they worked "so hard to build." Why she falls for this, I can't say. What I can say is that if she's committed to their marriage, she ought to at least use her leverage to demand that he stop humiliating her. It would be interesting to see what happens when he can't eat his cake and have it too, the way he does now.

4. Lifestyle/Image.

Here's one of my favorite jokes: A middle-aged man and his wife are having lunch in a nice restaurant. Pretty soon a beautiful young woman walks up to the table and kisses the husband. "Call me later," she says before leaving. Outraged, the man's wife asks who the hell that was. "My mistress," the man says. "Mistress?!" says the wife. "Well, then, I want a divorce." "All right, fine," says the husband. "Fine with me if you want to give up the trips to Europe, shopping at Bergdorf Goodman's, as well as the vacation home and society dinners." The wife is silent for a moment, then notices a pretty young woman she doesn't recognize with a man she does. "Who's that with Harry?" the wife asks. "Harry's mistress," the husband says. "Hmmm," the wife says, "our mistress is better looking than his." And so it goes. Marriages of convenience evolve when one spouse, usually the wife, can't find the strength to abandon the lifestyle or standard of living to which he or she had become accustomed. Take my friend "Alex" and his wife, for example. Alex is a wealthy man, and by wealthy I don't just mean a few million bucks. I mean, bucks up the wazoo. The guy has three homes, a yacht, a private plane, and butler — the whole enchilada. He's the kind of guy they make movies about, and in fact his marriage is the kind of mess they've been writing about since the novel was invented. For the 25 years that he and his wife have been together, she hasn't given him just one "get out of jail free" card; she's given him a whole deck, followed by a second and third when he used up the first and second. The man just can't keep it zipped up. It's amazing. I once asked him how he managed to pull it off, and he explained that they'd reached a sort of gentlemen's agreement: "I get to do whatever I want, and she gets to keep the lifestyle." What gets me, though, is that Alex has enough money to keep half a dozen people luxuriantly comfortable until the year 2525. Even after a divorce, his wife could live approximately the same lifestyle and avoid the embarrassment that has to go along with this not-so-secret secret. Of course, if she did leave him, she then wouldn't be in such close proximity to his considerable power. She'd rather suffer the humiliations, than cut off her source of what she considers her legitimacy. Sounds like

Hillary Clinton, doesn't it? No one who picked up a newspaper in the late 1990s didn't wonder, at least once, why the woman stayed with Bill. And we all probably came to the same conclusion: that for her, proximity to power, which she could then use as a fulcrum for her own ambitions, was more important than propriety; that her ends would justify her means. In fact, both Clintons were likely more concerned about their political image and future possibilities than they were about the sanctity of their marriage — and that was worth whatever ridicule they might have to endure. And Hillary especially was eager to sacrifice something in the present to get something bigger in the future. In short, theirs is the quintessential marriage of convenience.

5. Blame.

Women frequently remain in a bad marriage because they blame themselves somehow for the failure of the relationship; they rationalize that anything wrong their husbands do is warranted and justified — as if she "deserves" it. Naturally, her husband is likely to be a co-conspirator in this, as he probably offers constant reinforcement for her guilt. From what I've seen over the last decade, this feeling of guilt that the wife feels is more intense when she's a stay-at-home mom who hasn't earned income for years. She finds herself growing increasingly dependent on her husband for the material comforts of life, and at the same time less interesting and attractive. It's a ferocious and combustible mix. What she doesn't realize is that the marriage is alive in name only by that point. By the same token, there are also women who stay with abusive husbands because, once upon a time, the husband took care of them when they were sick, or because he bailed them out somewhere in the past; what's left is obligation, not love.

6. Religious beliefs.

Most organized religions aren't very tolerant of divorce, with Catholicism being the most famously intolerant. As a former altar boy myself (no, I wasn't abused), I have come to the conclusion that while I do believe in God, I do not necessarily believe in the Church and all its edicts. Its views on birth control and abortion are not, I believe, rationally defensible. But at least they're not laden with hypocrisy, as is its view on divorce. I'll never forget the time my friend Jim told me that he was flying to Rome solely to attend Mass at the Vatican. That this happened around the same time that I was losing my own faith made it seem all the more odd. Even so, I was happy for him, that he'd found his rock. Fast forward a few years to Jim's realization that his marriage had died; that happened, oh, around two years after he and his wife had stood on the pulpit and vowed in front of a priest that they would have, hold, and honor each other forever. Inconveniently for Jim, the Church frowned on divorce. Conveniently for the Church and Jim, Jim's bank account had an extra ten or twenty thousand bucks, allowing him to annul the marriage (which had already produced two children) and one day be married again by a priest in front of whom he and his wife will vow to stay together forever. But what of those people, unlike Jim, who can't afford to pay for an annulment? Personally, I can't imagine that God wants his children to suffer in cold, loveless, even abusive marriages. It's left to each of us to wake in the morning, look in the mirror, and decide what kind of life we're going to live. Popes, rabbis, imams, and pastors should have to wait outside, until we're done deciding.

I realize that some of you may find these six reasons overly simplified. Maybe they are. But with the exception of an illness requiring one partner to care for another, I haven't yet seen a marriage stick together for reasons that didn't fit somewhere in one or more of these categories. My attitude is that, at the core, marriage and life aren't really all that complicated; we add the complications ourselves when we preoccupy ourselves with what others will think of us if we do such and such. When it comes to a bad marriage, we need to think about ourselves first — what we're feeling and what we need. Only then will we find the strength, and clarity, to do the right thing.

Chapter 3

WILL WILLIS'S EIGHT
COMMON CAUSES FOR DIVORCE

Once people stop finding excuses to stay together, they generally don't have much difficulty ending the marriage. Divorced couples I've talked to always say that there was no single reason for the breakup; instead, it was a combination of reasons. Luckily, if you can spot and identify these reasons early enough and make the effort to correct the situation, you can actually avoid ...Will Willis's Eight Common Causes for Divorce.

Reason #1: *The Other Woman*

Once "the other woman" comes on the scene, it's usually impossible to consider that there might also be other reasons for the divorce. But in fact, "the other woman" (or even "the other man") is more than likely a symptom of hidden problems in the relationship that caused one partner to look elsewhere for something that was missing.

So, what was missing? What could have driven him into the arms of another?

First, it's important to understand that some women (some men, too, I suppose) actually *prefer* to date married men. Recently, a woman I was chatting with in an airport-waiting lounge told me about her fear of commitment — and in fact, she was on her way to meet her married boyfriend.

Why? I asked. Why wouldn't she want someone who was single, someone with whom she could build a life?

She explained that she preferred knowing that the relationship was doomed to go nowhere, and even laughed about her ex-boyfriend who'd left his wife and children to move in with her, only to move back home again three weeks later after she grew frightened and instigated a huge fight.

So that's one factor. Another is that some women, apparently, just want what you have. They want your husband. They want to take him from you and do not respect the sanctity of your home. They are without regard for the harm done to you and your children. They can only see what they see, and what they see is what they want, and what they want is what they have to have; in this way, they're like children.

Of course, it does indeed take a willing accomplice for affairs to bloom. Maybe the husband is experiencing some rough time emotionally and needs the kind of comfort that only a pair of big, innocent, puppy eyes can provide. Maybe he feels unappreciated or taken for granted and needs the kind of attention that can only be provided by someone who hasn't yet developed the sort of contempt that familiarity breeds. Maybe his wife has "let herself go" and he no longer feels attracted to her. There are a dozen or more possible factors at play here. But the point is that most men feel driven, by "good reasons," to have an affair.

Which brings us back to...*the other woman* as a symptom.

Happily married men who love their wives and children, and value what they have and don't want to lose it all, don't just wake in the morning and decide to have affairs. If you remember nothing else, remember that.

Reason #2: *We Grew Apart*

"We grew apart." That's the reason couples of all ages most often cite when asked to explain why they're divorcing. For example, couples that married while still in college sometimes find they "grew apart" when one of them had to work to support the other's graduate studies. Then there's the poor young lady who worked to put her husband through med school — only to have him leave her for a nurse because, in the words of the new doctor, "We grew apart." Meanwhile, it's almost become a cliché that the wife who stays home to care for the couple's children as her husband goes off to work will someday hear him shout down from high atop the corporate ladder how "we just grew apart."

No doubt you yourself know of or have experienced a story like one of these. And no doubt, in some cases couples actually do grow apart for otherwise good reasons. But in my opinion, the majority of growing-apart situations are avoidable. I believe that people grow apart because they've stopped trying to grow together. I'll give you an instance from my own life.

Early in my first marriage, my wife gave birth to a beautiful daughter, whom she doted on and wanted to stay home with. Unfortunately, like most young couples, we needed two incomes in order to make ends meet, so my wife still had to work weekends, when I myself was home and could stay with our daughter. You can see where this is going. We grew apart because we never focused on anything that might keep our relationship alive and fresh. In the little time we did spend together, my wife usually talked about what our daughter did that day. It's not that that wasn't important; it was. But like most men, I could only hear so much about the consistency of baby poop. I frankly wasn't interested in what she had to say.

Similarly, I'm sure my wife had to keep her eyes from glazing over whenever I told her how Joe had undercut Bob and fired Tom at the office — and that's if I bothered to tell her the details. I usually didn't, since the stress of living them the first time was bad enough without having to relive everything again at the end of the day.

Bottom line: We were losing what we'd had in common and didn't develop new common interests. We got lazy. We flat out stopped trying to keep our relationship growing. Which is, in the end, the death of relationships. In that way they're like sharks, as Woody Allen once pointed out. If they don't keep moving forward, they die.

Reason 3: *Personal Crisis*

Personal crises are hard to predict and even harder to prepare for. But here again, crises are usually symptoms, not causes.

Consider the case of the middle-aged man who's now unemployed, having lost his job in a corporate downsizing. You don't have to be a rocket scientist, or a reader of *Psychology Today,* to know it's a given that men fly through tremendous emotional turbulence after being fired; in general, they equate who they are with what they do.

If you're one of the five people on earth who doesn't believe that, prove it by asking a man, any man, to tell you about himself. You can bet the farm right now that he'll start with what he does for a living. Ask him to leave that part out of his comments and he'll invariably get tongue-tied.

That's why losing his job creates such emotional havoc, causing him to question his self worth — indeed, whether his life is worth anything at all. At the least he'll question his own manhood, and will sometimes try to prove he's still a man by taking little Elvis on a field trip.

This scenario is particularly relevant the more successful the man was — the higher he'd climbed on the corporate ladder

— before losing his job. It's the harder-they-come, harder-they-fall syndrome. A man who's lying on the pavement feeling like Humpty Dumpty will grab for anyone or anything to put him back together again.

If the marriage was strong when he fell, it will likely survive the crisis. But if the man was in anyway unhappy with his home life, this may be just the excuse he needs to further exaggerate the relationship's flaws as a way of "justifying" an affair. In other words, he'll conveniently blame his own crisis on his relationship in order to make himself feel better. He'll even rationalize getting out of the marriage as the discarding of excess baggage. I know about that, because I did it.

Once upon a time I lost a job and was so distraught I decided that what I needed was to simplify my life — you know, pare down my expenses and belongings; get rid of what I thought I didn't need. Though I was being paid nearly half a million bucks in severance, I still panicked about being out of work. *How long can I survive?* I kept asking myself while tossing and turning night after sleepless night. I cut every imaginable expense, canceling even the newspaper and cable TV. It was irrational, and it was stupid, and throughout that whole period I couldn't have felt more alone. My wife wasn't someone I could turn to for sustenance. She didn't work, didn't cook, didn't clean, and wasn't interested in sex; what she did do well was make dinner reservations.

As a consequence, I decided to move forward without the "extra burden" of her as my wife. Extra burden — that's how

I thought of her. I'm not proud of what I did, jettisoning her like deadweight on a boat in a storm. But I can comfort myself (a little) with the knowledge that our marriage would've ended sooner or later; it was a ship to nowhere, at least not with us aboard.

Another crisis that seems to cause men to reevaluate their lives is, not surprisingly, the death of their fathers. Because most men seem to go through life seeking Dad's approval, this phenomenon is true even if father and son weren't close and loving. No matter how Dad dies — whether it was sudden or following a protracted illness — men will react by asking themselves: "What's my life all about? Am I really happy? Is this how I want to live today, knowing I might die tomorrow?"

In answering those questions, a lot of men decide that happiness and satisfaction are being denied to them by a conspiracy — with their wives and the institution of marriage as co-conspirators.

Here, too, if the marriage was strong before Dad died, it will probably survive any second thoughts the son/husband might have about himself and his life. But if the relationship was weak, it could easily crumble under the resulting emotional pressure.

We must also pay homage to the most common cause of male crises — milestone birthdays. That's right. For some reason, when men turn 30, 40 50, 60, and 70, something happens to their brain, on account of what they think is happening to their bodies. They suddenly feel a need to prove that they still have their fastball and can hit the slider. Sadly, if you're not there cheering and pretending that he's yet worthy of Playgirl, there's a good chance he'll find someone who will. In short: Men are essentially insecure and are in need of constant positive reinforcement. True or not, they need to be told how wonderful they are — and believe that you still find them hunky and sexy.

Like it or not, the best way to deal with a man's personal crisis is to be sensitive and sympathetic to what he's going through. Even if you think it's just a concocted crock of garbage, you have to try to make him talk about his feelings and not allow him to isolate you from what he's experiencing emotionally. Recognize that, regardless of how strong he appears on the outside, inside he's as fragile as a child. He needs your support, your comfort, and yes, even mothering. Don't wait for him to ask for those things, because he probably doesn't even realize he needs them. He just knows that he needs something. And being a man, he probably thinks it's sex — with someone else.

Being a "partner" will go a long way toward getting you two through this crisis — together.

Reason #4: *Tired of the Same Old, Same Old*

Feeling tired of the same old stuff is sometimes mischaracterized as "growing apart." In reality, though, it's a different phenomenon. What people get tired of, and eventually want out from, is being ignored. And living with a nitpicker. And being interrupted when speaking. And being corrected, or edited, when telling a story. And being taken for granted or not appreciated. And having to work all day and then doing the shopping on the way home. And having to constantly pick up around the house after someone else. And giving a lot more than 50 percent, a hundred percent of the time.

There is, so far as I know; only one way to minimize all that accumulated fatigue. It's called communication.

Relationship partners have to be able to communicate their aggravation with each other in a non-hostile, even-tempered environment. Fact is, people aren't mind readers. Your partner can't possibly know what your complaints are unless you express them, nor can you know what your partner's complaints are unless you're told.

Now, what happens after the communication is exchanged will tell you whether or not your relationship has already fallen into the "growing apart" trap, soon to be followed, perhaps, by the "other woman." And, for God's sake, don't wait to communicate until you're already having a heated argument and are well into pointing out each other's flaws (see my note above re a "non-hostile, even-tempered environment"). This is the worst possible time to bring up what you're tired of; neither of you can possibly think rationally, nor at that moment are you all that eager to enhance your relationship. So pick and choose your time wisely, making sure that what you have to say is something you *both* need to work at in order to strengthen your relationship.

In thinking back to my own two marriages, I have to admit that the only times I ever talked about how "I felt" were

during heated arguments when I was already spewing bile —
which my wives would invariably remember, elephant-like, for
years afterward.

Also, never ever wait until you're in bed at night, both
of you exhausted from a long day, before starting a conversation
with those four deadly words, "We need to talk." You may as
well just stick an ice pick in his ear — and one up his nose for
good measure.

Feeling tired of the same old, same old should *never* be
the precipitating factor for a divorce or breakup. Once you accept
that every relationship has built-in ups and downs, you can accept
that they're opportunities to actually strengthen the bond between
you through solid communication. Lavishing on these down
moments the time, attention, and words that they deserve, will
fix the problems — which will stay fixed.

Reason #5: *Control Freak*

Everyone has had a close encounter with, or knows well,
a control freak. You know the type — someone who likes to tell
you what to wear, how to cut your hair, what to eat, what movie
to see, how to drive, etc. He manages the money without your
input, he carries all the assets in his name, he tells you how to
raise the children (and expects you to do it by yourself), then
treats you as if you were a child.

Generally speaking, the control-freak reason for a divorce
should be combined with the same old-same old and abuse

reasons. But I think it's important enough by itself to warrant its own discussion. It's also the easiest reason to identify, meaning that you can even spot it during the courting stage, when you're most able to get up from the table and leave. There's no question that if your potential partner is a control freak while you're dating, he'll be a super-control freak when you're married. Control freaks only get more controlling with age, usually because their negative behavior gets reinforced over time, making them progressively less flexible.

If you do find yourself dating a control freak, run — don't walk — for the nearest exit. Because believe me, as miserable as it is to be married to a control freak, divorcing one is even worse...and you will, eventually, get a divorce.

Reason #6: *Empty-Nest Syndrome*

Sadly, a lot of relationships end once the job — and distraction — of raising a family at home ends. Everyone, I'm sure, knows a couple who either divorced or stood on its precipice of divorce after their last kid went off to college.

Can you guess why this happens?

For some, it happens because the couple was staying together for the children's sake anyway. But most of the time it's because the couple is now facing each other directly for the first time in 20-something years — and they either don't like, or don't recognize, what they see.

No longer can they hide behind homework and soccer and prom dresses. Gone is the daily fretting over grades (and whether their kids will get into college). Now, the dinner table has just two places set, and no one else to carry the conversation. Will there be anything left to say?

In a way, it's like starting the relationship all over again, and when the two partners go out on that first date, they decide whether they want to see each other again. Well, all these years later, it's quite possible that one partner, if not both, may decide that this relationship has lost its legs. After all, this is a first date without the excitement, the romance, and the sexual tension; there are no secrets to be kept or revealed, no mysteries to unfurl. And now, all the little things that were lost or had gone unnoticed within the chaos of ordinary family life is suddenly the size of a billboard and flashing messages in Technicolor.

Meanwhile, both partners are facing the reality of getting older, knowing they've just crossed another bridge.

To say the least, relationships that haven't continued to grow and thrive all these past years are most vulnerable to breaking now. The only way to avoid this uniquely dangerous mix of feelings is to make sure that your relationship is the primary one in your household, the one that all the others revolve around. Feed it constantly with love and affection and vacations and dates so that you don't suddenly discover one sad fall morning that your children's parents are, at long last, strangers to each other.

Reason #7: *Physical or Mental Abuse*

No one, neither male nor female, should tolerate a single

instance of physical abuse. Never should the abused give the abuser a second chance. Never. Under no circumstances! Not for any reason! Okay?

Obviously, divorce is the only way out of marriage in which one of the spouses is an abuser. I know that sounds frightening. But no matter how painful divorce may be, isn't it better than the pain and terror of abuse? And don't you owe your children a safe home?

Physical abuse is a sickness for which there's no sure cure. Just as a heroin addict has to shoot more and more in order to get the same high, so too does an abuser have to get a little more physical each time.

The only response is to just leave. Leave after the first time…because there will always be a next time, no matter how contrite or anguished he seems afterward. Eventually the well of anger and outrage will fill back up, and you will once again be the target for what he thinks the world is doing to him.

And if you find yourself trying to rationalize his actions or making apologies for him, you are an "enabler" — that is, you enable him to abuse you. Please, if this describes you, get help; seek immediate counseling. Do it now.

All right?

Keep in mind too that, in its own way, mental abuse can be just as damaging as physical abuse. And its effects can be more insidious for being subtle.

So what is mental abuse? How is it defined?

In answering those questions, let me first point out that

our basic human nature is to be somewhat manipulative or controlling of our partners; it's how we get what we want from each other, and both sexes do it. Only when that manipulation becomes excessive, permeating every facet of the relationship, can it be considered abuse.

Brow-beating, carping, constant criticism, frequent rages, simmering anger, passive-aggressive behavior, remarks like "I'm going to leave you and you'll end up with nothing" and "You're lucky to have me, because no one else would put up with you" — these are all types or hallmarks of emotional abuse.

A woman I met recently through common friends told me an astounding story of emotional abuse. Her husband, she said, would sometimes get angry with her and disappear for a few days, then return without explanation — and in fact without a word at all; he wouldn't talk to her for weeks, taking up residence in the guest room until he felt good and ready to pretend he was married again. When I asked her why she tolerated such cruelty, she claimed she had no alternative. Her house, the cars, and all the marital assets were in his name. She didn't work, had no other means of support, and just accepted that this was the way things were.

For the victim, recognizing emotional abuse is frequently difficult. One reason is that she's likely to be someone with low self-esteem or a poor self-image, meaning that she may feel the abuse is deserved. It sometimes takes a friend to point it out to the victim, who of course will deny it until the day comes when the cumulative weight of taunts and insults is like a, well, bracing slap of reality.

To this woman I just described who tolerated her husband's disappearances and silent rages, I said almost exactly these words: "Snap out of it." She was an attractive woman in her mid-thirties, with no children to complicate the issue; there could be no excuse for tolerating such abuse. "You're an enabler," I said. "Go see an attorney tomorrow. Get the house appraised. Get a job. Get your own apartment. And get on with your life."

Some time later she called me, in tears — but they were tears of joy. "Thank you," she said. "I did exactly what you recommended, and now I can't believe I let that go on for so long. Thank you."

You're welcome.

A few final words on mental abuse. Most husbands aren't very good liars, in that they tell the truth in ways that they're not aware of themselves. So wives should always heed the wisdom of two otherwise common clichés: "Many a truth is said in jest," and "A drunken man's words are a sober man's thoughts."

Don't think for a minute that your partner's snide jokes or flip comments are meaningless, because they're not; they're actually his way of telling you something he can't find the words to tell you any other way. I know this, because that's what I used to do to my wife, "joking" that I'd just been to see my girlfriend. In fact, I had — and was unconsciously trying to tell her so, probably to relieve my guilty conscience.

As for drunken remarks, bear in mind that people like to say outrageous things when they're loaded, believing they can hide behind a mask of drunkenness and later deny that they meant the words that came out of their mouths. But in my experience the words represent the truth that slips out when the conscience is too drunk to notice. Example: Every time a friend of mine had a few drinks, he'd crack a couple of jokes about his wife's being overweight — and other women's great figures. He'd blame his rudeness on the booze (and so did she), but it was pretty clear to me that this was his way of trying to tell her something he didn't know how to say straight out — or straight.

Mental abusers aren't created overnight. Instead, they build over time, empowered by the acquiescence of their enabling mates. Try to spot the abuse early in your relationship, and move quickly to either stop it or leave before you've invested too much time in the relationship.

Reason #8: *Conflicting Priorities*

Relationships often dissolve when each partner wants something different from the other. At the beginning, yes, it's mostly sweetness and light, and you each ignite the love light in the other's eyes. But in time, as the newness wears off and life goes on, priorities change in ways that may not be synchronized. What's more, one partner's changing needs may become wholly unrealistic or unattainable.

Example: A young couple gets married, both of the partners hoping to achieve the traditional American Dream. The husband wants a successful business career. They both want a nice house, good cars, two kids, money for vacations, a college fund, and a hefty retirement nest egg. To get all that, the husband works longer and longer hours, pursuing his career with the aim of providing for his growing family's needs and responsibilities. Meanwhile, the wife focuses on creating the perfect home.

Slowly, imperceptibly, the partners' needs and wants begin to change over time — and neither one notices anything about the other's invisible plan. The first clue may start when the wife demands that her husband be home at a certain time each night, so he can start eating with her and the kids. The husband insists that that's not realistic; if he doesn't put in the extra hours, he'll never climb the ladder. They argue. She calls him selfish. He says he's only doing it "for the family." She claims she "never asked for all this." And on it goes. Vacations are postponed or canceled. Instead of more time at home, he actually begins spending less time, and misses teacher conferences, school plays, recitals, soccer games and more.

Obviously, this couple is heading toward marital disaster. You might say that they're "growing apart." But the growing-apart syndrome is characterized by laziness and disinterest. With conflicting priorities, the culprits are selfishness, naiveté, and an inability to communicate common goals and objectives. Growing apart can be avoided by finding common pursuits. Conflicting priorities aren't quite as easy to solve; readjusting the male drive from bigger better faster doesn't happen overnight, nor does altering the female nesting instinct. It ain't easy, that's for sure, but the only way out is through constant, loving, generous communication.

So there you have Will Willis's Eight Common Causes For Divorce. None of them is a standalone cause, and most divorces can be attributed to at least two causes. Relationships in which the partners are growing apart usually terminate with another woman or some form of mental abuse. Relationships where the partner is sick of the same old, same old are frequently abusive anyway — so can another woman be far behind? Then, too, any of these situations can be catalyzed by personal crises like milestone birthdays or the deaths of close friends and relatives.

In short, the explanations for why couples divorce are extremely complex and are anyway relevant only to the extent that they may help you to recognize that successful marriages are *not* based on some theoretical 50-50 distribution of contributions. More often than not, the ratio is something like 90-10. To live with that perceived inequality, you've got to be willing to maintain honesty and openness with your partner, and work at the relationship every day. If you don't, it may be only a matter of time until one or more of the above reasons bite you in the butt as you sit waiting in divorce court.

Next up: How to spot the signs of, or avoid, affairs in a marriage.

Chapter 4

HOW TO HAVE AN AFFAIR-FREE MARRIAGE

No doubt you've heard the axiom, "If you want to have a friend, then be a friend." Truer words have probably never been spoken. So it only follows that if you want to *have* a good partner, you need to *be* a good partner.

Marital relationships rely on mutual attraction, common interests, and shared goals. But they're actually built on friendship. That's why couples who love each other but aren't otherwise friends tend to break up more frequently and more easily than those who have their friendship to fall back on when, over time, the heat of passion starts to cool.

Let's bring the issue close to home. Start by thinking about your best friend. What makes your relationship a "best"? My guess is that total trust and complete freedom to be yourselves are somewhere in the top three of attributes, with the third being your support and encouragement of each other's lives and goals. You look forward to and enjoy being together, you share common interests, you'd sacrifice almost anything for each other, and, probably, you make each other laugh. Would you do anything to hurt your best friend? No, not intentionally, and if you did, you'd feel terrible and apologize at once.

Now think of your spouse. Do the same criteria hold for your marriage, and how you feel about him? If the answer is no, then some serious reassessment is in order. Is the problem with you? Or is it with him? Maybe it's with both of you. And maybe the relationship is suffering because of it.

If you fear that your spouse is turning away from you instead of toward you, it's probably time to do a little investigating as a way to ease your mind (an uneasy mind begins playing tricks on its owner, possibly leading to irrational behavior down the line as the madness builds).

Begin by understanding that, according to the latest research studies, over 55 percent of all married men eventually will succumb to the temptations of sex outside of their marriage. That's the bad news.

The good news is that men are basically lazy. In my not so humble estimation, if cheating is easy for them, they'll probably do it. But, if it's difficult, and there's a high probability of getting caught and suffering the consequences, they're less likely to fool around on the side.

"A man's faithfulness is directly proportional to his

options," was the comment I once heard a comic make. As sad as that sounds, there's probably a lot of truth in it. But don't for a minute think that, just because your husband is fat, balding, and dresses like Willy Loman, he's safe from the clutches of some home wrecker. On the other hand, just because he looks like Mel Gibson doesn't mean he's out playing Casanova, either.

Please understand, I'm not suggesting that you get yourself a deerstalker hat and pipe and pretend to be Sherlock Holmes. What I am suggesting is that you remain utterly and completely vigilant when it comes to your husband's free time —the "who", what, when, where, and how of his leisure. Turning a blind eye to his whereabouts, and refusing to believe even that his straying is a possibility, should not be an option for you. Women who do that suffer from what I call the Tinker Bell Syndrome. Do you remember Peter Pan and Tinker Bell? What women suffering from the Tinker Bell Syndrome believe is that all they have to do to make what they want come true, is to close their eyes, believe real hard, and clap their hands. Not only will Tinker Bell come back to life, but their husbands will turn into Ward Cleaver. It's like the old Richard Pryor joke about his wife catching him in bed with another woman. Immediately, he denies it. "But I saw you," she says. To which he replies: "Who you gonna believe, me or your own lyin' eyes?"

I remember once coming home in the middle of the night smelling like a French whore, and my wife accepting some totally lame excuse without even challenging me. She just didn't want to accept the fact that something was wrong with our relationship. In other words, she didn't want to believe what she didn't want to believe. The same thing happened with the weekend fishing trips I took "with my friends." She knew damn well that I wouldn't know which end of a fishing pole to hold, but it was easier and cleaner for her to hide from reality than to question what was really happening to her marriage.

Now look, just because there are a lot of philandering jerkoffs like I was out there doesn't mean that every fishing trip or late-night venture your husband takes is worthy of paranoia. Not all of us men are as mindlessly obvious as I was. In fact, I didn't get so brazen with my behavior until I was ready for the marriage to end anyway. By then, I *wanted* to get caught. I *wanted* my wife to confront me. I *wanted* her to say something. Sadly, she never did, though it wouldn't have mattered if she had; by then there was nothing worth saving between us.

To help you discern the difference between what you fear, what you ought to fear, what you're imagining, and what you're not seeing, I'm going to give you some telltale hints to look for in a man who presumably hasn't yet reached the point where he wants to get caught; this is the time when something good and positive might yet come from your pro-active attitude.

If you do suspect your husband of cheating, do *not* immediately confront him. Nor should you tell a friend, because your friend will invariably tell her husband, and, well, you get the drill. At the beginning, at least, you don't want him to know that you're suspicious. It will only make him more careful about covering his tracks, so you'll never confirm the truth. For a while, let him think he's getting away with something. The longer he does it, the lower his defenses will be, and the sloppier he'll act in trying to hide what needs hiding. However, here are a few things to look for:

The Wandering Eye: Does your husband have an inappropriately wandering eye? When you're out in public, say, at a restaurant, does he focus more on other women in the joint than he does on you? I know, I know, and you know, too, that every man looks at other women ("I'm married, I'm not dead," I once heard a man explain to his wife). But is your husband *obsessed* with looking at other women? Does he have to flirt with every decent-looking woman, regardless of the situation? And if a male friend is present, does he motion or make comments and gestures to him about every woman within view?

I have a male acquaintance that even makes me uncomfortable with his behavior. He'll get up from the table and walk to the bar to get drinks, just so he can check out other women. It's comical the way he'll almost fall out of his chair — unintentionally — watching a pretty woman go by. Why his wife puts up with that kind of behavior, I don't know.

In your marriage, you have to ask yourself whether your husband's actions make you feel uncomfortable. Do they embarrass you? Humiliate you? If so, there's likely a problem either brewing or ready for bottling. React by having a calm conversation with him in which you describe your discomfort and how it makes you feel. Then, listen to what he says in response (The correct answer is an apology and a promise to correct his behavior). However, just as importantly, watch to see what he does. Actions, as always, speak louder than promises. If his behavior doesn't change, or doesn't stay changed for long, you are undoubtedly looking at serious trouble in your marriage. A man who is totally insensitive to his wife's feelings has probably lost his affection for her. Either that, or he's an incorrigible jerk.

Newfound Vanity: Does he suddenly develop an interest in trying to look good again, after years of not caring?

True, most every man harbors at least a little vanity; very few get up in the morning without a care for the face they present to the world. But the question here is, has he developed a mysterious passion for working off or dieting off that beer belly and "love handles"? Has he gotten a new hairstyle or bought some Rogaine for the bald spot that's been there for years? Has he gone from dressing like a preppy to wearing Italian leather? Does he check the size of his muscles every time he passes a mirror? Is he trying new cologne after years of the same fragrance?

If the answer is yes to one or more of these questions, it's time for a reality check. The bottom line is that men who are comfortable in their marriages generally don't develop sudden concerns about their weight and fitness level (unless, of course, it's a result of the doctor's edict). Take me, for example. I went from green corduroys with red lobsters on them to Italian silk slacks, Gucci shoes, and slicked back hair (like Pat Riley). Was that a signal to my wife? Yeah, it was. Did she see it? No, she didn't. Did the marriage end badly? Well, you know the answer to that.

Work Habits: Does your husband suddenly start working longer hours than he used to? Does he now have unexpected weekend trips? Is he at the office later into the night than usual? Does he leave for work earlier than necessary? If he's an hourly worker, does his paycheck reflect the overtime he says he put in? (Do you even see his paycheck?) Is it hard to reach him when he's working after hours?

When I was younger I had a boss who worked every weekend — or so he told his wife. He knew he could take advantage of the office building's security and its phone system, which made it impossible for her to show up unexpectedly or contact him by phone (this was before cell phones). So he managed to avoid getting caught in one of his little trysts until his wife cornered his boss at a holiday party and complained about how unfair it was to the family that her husband had to work all those late nights and weekends. Hmmm, said the boss. And, within a week, my boss got a double whammy: he lost both his job and his wife. Neither the wife nor his boss appreciated how creatively he was using his office sofa.

More questions: Do you study your husband's travel itinerary? Are return flights frequently delayed or canceled? (If Delta were as bad as I made them out to be, the airline would've been out of business years ago.) Is he not in his hotel room during normal sleeping hours? Does he complain about last-minute hotel changes? Any late-night secretive phone calls from his home office? Does he make calls from phone booths, even when he has his cell phone? Does he walk outside with his cell, so as "not to disturb you"? Does he make outgoing calls on his fax line (meaning that the person calling him back — the other woman, who probably doesn't know he's married — can only get that annoying fax beep)? Are you getting a lot of "Sorry, wrong number" calls (which begin when the other woman learns that he is married, and gets her hands on his real phone number)?

Still more: Do you have access to all of his access codes, like email or voicemail passwords? If not, why not? If so, have you ever read his deleted emails? You see, by cutting off his easy access to communication with her, it's much harder for him to develop their relationship.

How about credit card charges and monthly invoices? Do you ever study them? (Seeing charges at Victoria's Secret, if you haven't gotten any presents from there, isn't a good sign.) Is he opposed to your opening things addressed to him? If so, why? Does he receive most of his personal mail at the office or at a PO box? Why? And do you ever catch him not wearing his wedding ring? (You can believe it if he says it cuts off his circulation; his circulating around in the bars!)

Does he suddenly find reasons to go out late at night for, say, an exotic flavor of chewing gum that they only have at a certain store in Philadelphia — and you live in Pittsburgh? (I knew a guy who took up smoking just so he could go out for cigarettes and call his girlfriend.)

How about poker nights or softball nights or bowling nights? Do you know that's where he really is? Have you ever happened by the country club (or bowling alley) and noticed that his car wasn't there when he supposedly was having his weekly game? (That supposedly weekly round of golf gave me a full five hours every Sunday to practice my stroke.)

All right, enough questions. The points are simple enough: There are literally countless ways and opportunities for your husband to cheat on you, if that's his inclination. To check on him every second, you'd need a private investigator. Some women do go that route. So let's say you're one of them, and you do hire a P.I.; there are two possible outcomes: One, hubby is caught cheating and you have the evidence to prove it. Two, he's not cheating and you feel better. If he is cheating, you have the choice of either confronting him (probably ending up in divorce court), or of not confronting him and living with the constant heartache of knowing that your husband isn't really your husband anymore. Then, too, there's the possibility of your non-cheating hubby finding out that you had him followed. He's likely to be furious — and I guarantee you that he won't believe your line about how he should be flattered by your interest in him.

So what's the moral? Relationships are a delicate balance between caution and trust, and they're far easier to fix *before* the other woman confuses literally everything.

Chapter 5

COMMON MYTHS/LIES TOLD DURING A DIVORCE

Anger, fear, and panic are the dominant emotions on display during a divorce. Consequently, deception comes in to play, too.

Depending on the circumstances and the final objectives, divorcing partners will say just about anything they think will ease their guilt, release their anger, and get them what they want — as quickly as they can. And much of what they say is as truthful as "the check's in mail." So if you are, unfortunately, going through the process of a divorce, here's where you need to check your naiveté at the door and listen with skepticism.

#1
"We'll still be friends."

At some point, even during the ugliest divorce, one partner will turn to the other and, in a voice dripping with honey, say that he hopes they'll still be friends after the divorce. Sure — and I have this bridge for sale also.

Listen, this guy is telling you that he doesn't want you in his life. Period. He's telling you he doesn't want to give you anything in the settlement. Period. He wants you to walk away with nothing. End of story. You're getting a divorce, remember? You're fighting over every dollar, every CD, every end table and kitchen knife. Cruel, vicious things are being said every day, and spotlights suddenly illuminate each of your worst sides. Don't fall for his lines. And anyway, why would you even *want* to be friends with this jerk? He's still trying to manipulate you. The best you can do, if kids are involved, is to be civil — so that you can maintain a workable relationship as the kids grow. But if kids aren't involved, don't be afraid to look him straight in the eye and say, "Friends with you? I'd rather have root canal without Novocain." Believe me, the chances of you and your ex ever having a successful post-marital friendship are about on par with winning the Lotto. Expect the worst and, if by chance, a friendship someday develops through mutual desire, then consider yourself incredibly lucky. Trust me, if your soon-to-be ex really wanted to be your friend, he'd have worked harder to make the marriage work.

#2
"It's not you, it's me."

I love this line, maybe because all of us have used it sometime as an excuse to break off a relationship that was going nowhere and we didn't know how to tell the truth. Sure, we were trying to spare someone's feelings, but when you think about it, it's a ridiculous ploy. Consider: I'm leaving you, so I tell you that the problem is me…and you're going to go, "Whew, that was a close one. I thought it was me." I don't think so. In fact, the only person who's going to feel better is the person who utters the phrase — if he gets away with it. Don't let him. And anyway, it's not doing either of you any good to avoid the truth at a time like this. When it comes to divorce, you know damn well whose fault it is. In fact, if he does say, "It's not you, it's me," you can snap back with, "You're right. It is you. So give me everything I want."

#3
"The divorce will not get ugly, I promise."

Great line. I remember when my ex-wife and I agreed to have a calm and rationale divorce — you know, the height of civility and graciousness; no name calling, no hostility, no ratting each other out to other people, reasonable and equitable in the division of assets. Right. As the poet once said, "The best-laid plans of mice and men go awry." Our pledge lasted, oh, two minutes. And you know why? Because divorces are painful. They're the salt that gets poured on the open wounds of your relationship. The stress of suddenly having to face reality after months or years of willfully ignoring it, hurts a lot and sends your moods on an out-of-control roller coaster ride. Words are said in anger that may have been locked up for a long time and are, at the least, exaggerated by all the accumulated emotion. You let it out any way you can, even by talking to people you don't know. I remember my ex-wife telling airline passengers in the seats next to her what an a-hole I was, and about all the awful things I did to her. (Can you imagine having to sit next to this woman and listen to her rage all the way from Miami to San Francisco? Yikes. I pity the poor bastards.) Then, once attorneys get involved and turn up the heat, the situation usually goes from miserable to intolerable. That, in fact, is one of the tools an effective divorce attorney uses to get you what you want. Your ex will do anything to stop the torture.

Now, all that having been said, it's important to try to keep the ugliness to a minimum, because in later years (especially if children are involved), you're likely to feel ashamed or embarrassed by how foolishly you acted. And you certainly don't want to do anything that harms your young children; they'll never forget or forgive you, no matter how deserved you believe your actions are. So to the degree that you can contain your emotions — and tongue — try to focus on the ultimate objective: getting the divorce completed and moving on with your life. The best revenge is to live well.

#4
"I'll give you anything you want."

This is a good thing to hear, but don't fall for it. Early in the divorce process, men who are leaving women usually feel ashamed and will say just about anything to get women to stop crying and suffering emotionally. Well, if he really wanted to spare your feelings, he'd be a good husband, not a petitioner. Trust me, as the process goes on, you'll see how fast his tone changes. However, if he utters those "I'll give you anything you want" words, quickly get a pad and pen and commit it to writing. It's not legally binding, but it will stop the bullshit.

#5
"There's no need to put it in writing."

Another common lie. Men promise to lasso the moon if they think it might get them laid, so it's wise to ignore any promise that's not in writing with a signature attached. I remember speaking with a woman who told me that her husband promised to pay for their kid's private school but wouldn't allow it into the divorce settlement. Result? Public school. Moral? Verbal promises aren't worth the carbon dioxide they're written in.

#6
"There isn't anyone else."

Right. And I swear I thought she was eighteen.

Men seem to think that women will feel better if the divorce is a result of good old-fashioned failure — that you failed as a wife — rather than home wrecking. In other words, women should take comfort in knowing that other women weren't better than they were. Dumb, dumb, dumb. Personally, I think it's a case of projection. Men who lose their wives to other men worry that they don't measure up, lengthwise, in the equipment department. As I said, dumb. Anyway, a man who says there's no other woman, without being asked, is probably volunteering too much. Translation: there's another woman. You can count on it.

Now, in truth, the other woman may have come along after the fact, when the marriage was over in every way but legally. She may have been the catalyst who made him believe that divorce was the right thing to do, and that there was a bottomless ocean of beautiful single women waiting to skinny dip with him. That's quite a catalyst — and it's going to be quite a rude awakening for him some day. But that's beside the point. What he likely wants, in telling you that there isn't anyone else, is to avoid seeing your discomfort. So he lies. What's one more lie in a series?

Bottom line: If he tells you there's not another woman, ignore him and get on with the business of divorcing. In regard to the divorce process, the absence or presence of another woman is totally irrelevant anyway. Most states have "no-fault" divorces, so it doesn't matter if you have photos of him with a goat! The divorce and settlement process is the same.

#7
"I won't see her anymore."

He'll yank this one out of nowhere after he's been caught with his pants down — but hasn't yet made the ultimate decision to divorce. If you still love him at all and want to work things through, you'll be inclined to believe him. And you will believe him. But that doesn't mean you don't need marriage counseling immediately. You do. Insist on it; insist that he show up at a where, when and with a *who* of your choosing. You'll find out whether there's anything left to save in the marriage. But while you're finding out, protect yourself. Don't be naïve. Use your advantage of his (probably temporary) contriteness to shorten his leash, and keep close tabs. (Study all of my tips outlined in Chapter Four for having an affair-free marriage.) But most importantly, see an attorney — immediately. In preparing the groundwork for a divorce settlement — which you may or may not get to — the attorney will help you raise your level of skepticism about everything your husband tells you. Now is the time you have the most leverage. Use it. Get the lawyer to draft a document that will have your cheating husband suffering severe financial consequences in the event that he continues to see the "her" that he's not supposed to see anymore. It's a good way to find out how real his promise really is.

Remember, you're fighting to save your marriage, and you're allowed to use whatever tools are at your disposal. Like fear — his fear of destitution, for one. To win, you have to suppress all of your anger and hurt and fear, and channel those feelings into formulating a cohesive, winning plan. This is no time to go wobbly, as Maggie Thatcher once warned the first President Bush. After a month or so of life being seemingly back to normal, which is about the time he'll think he's out of the doghouse, hire a P.I. to follow him for a week. The small amount of money it costs is really an investment. Either you'll get the kind of peace of mind you'd never otherwise have (always worrying whether he's stepping out), or you'll find that he's not worthy of you and you can divorce him. Either way, you win.

#8
"The kids will adjust fine."

Uh-huh, and they lived happily ever after, too. Not!

Sure, kids are resilient. And yes, most kids have friends with divorced parents, so they can see that life goes on after Mom and Dad split. But kids are just that — kids. They don't have the coping mechanisms that adults do, and they don't have any control over the situation they're being thrust into. It's scary that their parents who brought them into the world together suddenly won't be a unit anymore. As a balm, they need constant attention and reassurance. "Mommy and Daddy still love you," is something they need to hear from both of you every day. "This doesn't change anything about that. We will always love you." And because children think the world revolves around them, you have to make clear that "You are not not not not the reason that we're getting divorced."

Please be acutely aware of how you and your soon-to-be ex act around each other when the kids are present. It's likely that they've already heard the two of you say some terribly unkind things to each other in the previous months, if not years, so now is the time to minimize the damage you've done. Don't wait until the decree is final; the kids won't believe anything from you by then. No, you've got to get with your husband and agree to keep as much ugliness from the eyes and ears of the kids as possible. They don't need to hear you tell stories about him, or hear from him everything you've done wrong. You may be absolutely right in everything you say, but this is your kids' father you're talking about, and they'll hate you forever for throwing darts at him.

#9
"Since we both love our kids, we'll do what's best for them and won't use them as 'pawns' or 'bargaining chips'."

This is the line that both of you should say to each other as you keep your children's welfare in mind. The problem is, it's too important a thought to be believed without verification. You may very well keep to your end of the deal, but when things get tough and ugly, your husband will probably succumb to the temptation to bring out the heavy guns.

And so will you. Believe me, you will.

Your attorney will point out that increased visitation is the best bargaining chip you have to increase monthly payments, so you'll say sure, go ahead, rationalizing that the kids will benefit. Divorce is a war, and war is ugly, and truth is its first casualty.

At some point you will come to accept the fact that the kids are going to be part of the negotiations, so your job then will be to minimize the damage done to them in the process. The less they hear (see above) what's going on, the better. And the fewer times you use them to act as your messenger, the better. I remember when my five-year-old daughter asked me why I wouldn't give her mother more money so that she could get a pony. I can't tell you how tempted I was to lay out in intricate detail how manipulative her mother could be, but I instinctively knew better than to try to explain the divorce settlement to a little kid.

Bottom line: Keep the kids out of the line of fire. It's dangerous enough back in the barracks with a war going on.

#10
"There won't be any lingering hate, anger, or hostility after the divorce is final."

Right, and the pope's a Baptist.

Let's stick with the war metaphor. In war, there is a winner and a loser — and losers don't like losing. For every negotiated point in the settlement, there'll be one side that's happier than the other. If a custody battle was waged, one side got what he or she wanted; rarely are there compromises. If alimony is involved, one side is getting something that the other side didn't want to give up, or conversely isn't getting something she deserves. If there was a material division of assets, somebody is going to look at his share of the pile and feel screwed. And so it goes.

In short, divorce proceedings are not win-win situations. "She got the gold mine and I got the shaft" is how the country song sums things up. The writer doesn't sound to me like a guy without lingering hate, anger, or hostility. In fact, I may as well have written that song myself. I remember how my blood would boil every month when I had to write a support check. And every time I picked up my daughters for the weekend, one of them would be holding an envelope in her little hand. Not once did they contain photos or drawings or samples of their schoolwork. Instead, they contained bills my ex wanted me to pay. All these years later, the bad feelings boil up in me when I think on those things too long. It's fine and good to say that bad feelings won't remain, but they will. Your job is to accept reality and move on as best you can.

#11
"My attorney wants what's best for both of us."

Yeah, and he's doing it for free, too.

This is one of those lines that's so seductive, you're dying to believe it. Don't. Not for a second. Your husband is paying his lawyer to represent him, not you. If the lawyer represents you on your husband's dime, your husband's going to feel like a sucker. Besides, the lawyer is legally obliged to protect his client, not his client's adversary; he can actually be disbarred for not offering a vivid advocacy of his client. And almost as severe, the lawyer's not going to get any referrals from your husband. Who, after all, would refer a nice-guy lawyer to a friend who's out for blood?

So don't get duped. Listen to *your* attorney — who wants what's best for his own client. You!

#12
"We'll use the same attorney to save money."

Men, trying to save a few bucks and some aggravation,

will frequently try to suggest this. I myself, for example, once uttered the words — and felt the blast of their backfire. What happened was that my wife allowed me to get a settlement agreement drafted by an attorney and then, on the sly, took it to her attorney for review. So the settlement I thought we were simply committing to paper turned out to be her attorney's starting point for negotiations. It was a major screw-up on my part (though I frankly did admire my wife's cleverness), and if you can pull off something similar when and if the time comes, more power to you.

Unless you have absolutely no assets and no children, and nothing is being contested, you'll need and want separate attorneys. But even then, using the same attorney can hurt you badly, as a friend of mine's wife was when he caught her cheating on him. Devastated, he filed for divorce; and guilt-ridden, she agreed to use the same attorney, even though the lawyer disclosed that the husband had retained him. The woman walked away from everything — house, cars, furniture, and all assets — and even split the liabilities. There's no way the outcome would've been the same if she'd hired her own attorney, no matter how guilty she felt. The bottom line here is to hire the shark, even if you're as contrite as a guppy.

#13
"We'll use a family friend as our attorney to save money."

Sure, go ahead, if you want him to be an ex family friend.

Family friends shouldn't act as lawyers for the same reason that surgeons don't operate on their own family members: there's too much emotion involved to think clearly. Besides, what's the good of having a lawyer who won't be your advocate? Family friends will feel obliged to act impartially, and that's not at all what you want. You want aggression. You want contained fury. You want someone who can look at your husband with contempt, not compassion. You want someone to act as your champion, not your husband's therapist. You want to win, not break even. And you don't want to lose a friend, you're going to need all you have after the divorce.

#14
"Our common friends will remain both of our friends after the divorce."

And the Chicago Cubs are going to win the World Series. Sorry, ain't gonna happen.

This is frankly one of the most upsetting things following a divorce. Just at the time when you could really use the love and attention of intimate companionship, you find that the friends themselves tend to choose sides. No doubt you've heard the quip that would be funny if it weren't true about the wife who got custody of the children and the husband who got custody of the friends.

Actually, it's women who usually win the "couple friends" — the ones they made together — and if the wives are close, the husbands will usually stop seeing each other.

I remember that during my second divorce, when I could've used a friend worse than New Englanders need sun in January, it was like I had leprosy. My male friends couldn't stay far enough away. And to make matters worse, they would side with their wives about what a creep I was and how they never saw "that side of me before." Huh? These were the guys I was prowling with all those years. Which reminds me: If your husband makes a big deal about a friend's divorce, your antenna should shoot straight up. The man who protests too much probably has something to hide. You may want to think back to the number of golfing or fishing trips the guys took together.

#15
"Your lifestyle will not change after the divorce."

Men like to tell their soon-to-be exes, and in fact they may believe, that there's not going to be a sudden, negative change in her lifestyle. But by definition, that can't be true. As an institution, marriage originally began as more or less of a financial arrangement; it benefited both parties to share a common roof and serve each other. And in fact, statistics show that married couples are more likely than single people to accumulate wealth over the long haul. So obviously, a change in marital status equates with a change in lifestyle.

Then, too, you're now much more likely to find yourself alone, or to have to go by yourself to parties and other social events. You have to make child-rearing decisions without help most of the time. What happens is, you drop the baggage of being married — and pick up the baggage of being single.

Bottom line: Your lifestyle *will* change. It's a lot easier to handle, though, if you expect it and accept it. Then you can prepare for it. Just keep in mind that millions before you have survived the ordeal. You will too.

#16
"We'll just separate for a while to give us some time to get our heads straightened out."

Personally, I've never understood the logic of a legal separation, unless the law required it. (Some states mandate that a couple live apart for 90 days before a divorce can be filed. Some states, believe it or not, prohibit you from having any sexual relations with your spouse 90 days prior to the divorce. Even if that law applied to either of my divorces, and it didn't, I wouldn't have had a problem keeping away. Apparently, though, some people do. But what does it say about a couple who hates each other in every other way but stay together because of sexual compatibility? Not much, I guess.)

To me, legal separations aren't logical. If you can't work things out when you're together, how the hell can you work it out when you're apart? It's nonsensical and illogical.

Unfortunately, when one spouse suggests separating for a while, it usually means he or she has somewhere else to go — and someone to go there with.

That's why I don't think separations do anything other than make things worse. Better to go straight to divorce court, as a friend of mine should have done some years ago. He'd asked his wife for a trial separation to "get my head together," meaning he wanted to spend some more time with his girlfriend before deciding whether he really wanted to divorce. His wife agreed, and when he was away she, too, began dating — and really enjoying the attentions of some very nice men. Meanwhile, though, my friend's girlfriend wasn't quite so lovely to him anymore, and he decided to come back. Oops. By then his wife wasn't interested in him. My friend went wild with jealousy (I guess he didn't see the irony), and the divorce got about a dozen times uglier than it would've been from the beginning.

Bottom line: don't waste your time with legal separations unless the law insists. And never take your husband's suggestion that you move in with your parents or friends for a while. That's called "abandonment" and it will negatively impact your settlement negotiations. If someone has to go, it should be him! And if you can get him to move out, without a formal separations agreement, you'll actually have a lot more leverage in divorce court. He would have abandoned you!

#17
"Marriage counseling will fix our marriage."

Well, maybe. Maybe more than maybe. Indeed, I believe strongly in marriage counseling — that is, if it's done early enough in the relationship. And...if both of you are equally committed to saving the marriage.

There are, though, a few things to keep in mind about counseling. First, it can't be successful if one of you is doing it simply to shut the other person up. I remember when an old friend took his wife to counseling at ten in the morning, and his girlfriend to lunch at noon. He was just going through the motions and wasting a lot of time and money.

Second, you have to be sure that the counseling is intended to repair the relationship, not provide the basis for the divorce. Example: I once sought marriage counseling just so I could hear myself say out loud, to a supposedly neutral third party, how miserable I was and how much I wanted out of my marriage. Ultimately, the counselor prescribed divorce. You see? It works.

A friend of mine recently tried counseling. Unfortunately, the husband was only interested in using the sessions as a means to attack all of his wife's flaws. His problems and weaknesses were totally off limits. Once again, counseling helped them to realize that they weren't meant for each other. It worked. They are now getting divorced.

Bottom line: Marriage counseling is a lot like marriage; it's only as successful as the effort each of you put into it.

#18
"Next week is going to get better."

Sounds like the last line from "Gone With The Wind," doesn't it?

Men say things like that — focusing on the future — because it allows them to avoid the dealing with the pain of the present. But like the proverbial dark before the dawn, you can count on things probably getting a lot worse before they get better. So don't fall for the line. Even if he can't, you need to deal with the present and assume that the best you can hope for is that things won't get *unbearably* bad. (They won't.) Anyway, things won't get better until he's out of your life and you've proven to yourself that you can make it alone. (You can.) Then, and only then, will things get better next week.

#19
"Let's have another baby to rekindle our love."

There are stupid ideas (like communism), and really

stupid ideas (like racism). And then there are ideas that are beyond being really, really, really stupid. Like having another baby when the marriage is in trouble.

It's such a bad idea that flushing all of your money down the toilet, torching the house, and living homeless on Skid Row are, by comparison, acts of genius. There is no possible way that adding a new baby to a bad marriage is going to result in a happy home.

Look, maybe, just maybe, if the couple doesn't have any other children, the suggestion can be excused on the grounds of ignorance. But the operative word above is "another," implying that ignorance is no excuse. If you already have children, and your marriage is going poorly, how in the world could you possibly imagine that another wailing pair of lungs, a hungry mouth, and dirty diapers will bring you closer? I remember when my wife and I were having problems after our first daughter was born. Against my better judgment, my wife convinced me that we could solve these problems with another kid. Well, the surprise turned out to be not one pair of wailing lungs but two; she had twins. And two years later, we were divorced. These poor girls were the unfortunate casualties of a bad decision — one that I knew I shouldn't be making. I knew early in our marriage that my wife and I were heading for a divorce, and we should've been, long before we stayed together long enough to create two more casualties of divorce.

What's even worse was how much more complicated and ugly the divorce procedure got because of now not just one child but three.

Bottom line: Be your children's parents, not their patients. They're not therapists.

#20
"I'm a good father."

Not long ago there was a story much in the news about a homeless woman who lived in her car with her sometime boyfriend and infant daughter. Sadly, the daughter bled to death after being bitten repeatedly by a rat that had taken up residence in the car, too. When the woman faced the judge on a charge of second-degree murder, she shouted out, "I'm a good mother." I've never forgotten that, if only as a way to illustrate how much distance there usually is between how we think of ourselves and how we really are.

A man who feels the need to declare "I'm a good father" when you're fighting him over not sharing in the child-rearing duties, probably protests too much. Just because he gives you (theoretically) plenty of money doesn't make him a good father — not if he's oblivious of the thousand other small acts that go into raising a child well. Like attending parent-teacher nights. Like making it a point to be there for the child's school events. Like taking time to help with homework. Like being there when the kids are sick. Like reading to them. Like talking to them about everything and nothing. Like being interested in their interests. Like saying "sure," when they ask to be taken somewhere. Like helping them to learn to solve life's problems by working them through together.

There's a lot more to being "a good father" than opening a wallet wide enough. And in my opinion, any man who says he's a good father probably doesn't have a clue about the other stuff. But if he insists, make him share in the weekday battles, too, not just the fun stuff on weekends. Teach him to be a good father by letting him see what a good mother does.

I'm sorry to say that you're likely to hear some, most, or even all of the above lines as you go through the divorce process. Remember that they're only lines, though; they're not true. And it's up to you not to get fooled by whatever emotional pleas and manipulations he pulls out of his bag of tricks. In Nancy Reagan's immortal words, "Just say no."

Chapter 6

HOW TO SELECT AN ATTORNEY

Once you decide that divorce is your last and only alternative, the most important decision you're likely to make is which attorney to hire. In fact, it's a pretty good idea to talk with a lawyer even *before* you've decided to divorce, not necessarily to dissuade you from your decision, but to give you some insights that only he (or she) could have, given that there's no situation he hasn't already seen. Example: Let's say you're thinking about going back to work or school in order to learn a new job skill you'll need to support yourself. Well, the attorney may suggest waiting to begin your studies until after the divorce is final, because if you've been out of work for some time, you may be entitled to alimony while you get educated to go back to work, whereas you may not be if you're gainfully employed. (Every state is different.)

Other factors, too, like the length of the marriage and the number of children affect the complexity of the settlement, and in fact may allow you to dispense with the whole nasty business by signing a do-it-yourself document downloaded off the Internet. But you'll only know how much legal help you need by talking to a legal advisor.

While money may play a large role in which pair of shoes you buy, don't skimp on a divorce attorney; it could come back to bite you later, in that expensive attorneys are expensive for a damn good reason: they're worth every penny, as their happy clientele will quickly attest. You don't shop for the cheapest doctor, do you? No, you search for the best. Anyway, the courts will probably require your husband to pay your legal expenses — and that's regardless of who's "at fault" (most states now have no-fault divorces in order to avoid swamping the court docket with ugly battles over who cheated on whom, etc.)

The best example I can give you for how not to select an attorney is the way I did it for my first divorce. I made the mistake of assuming that the split was going to be amicable, and that we were simply going to divide up everything before saying hasta la vista. So it didn't seem necessary to spend a lot on a lawyer (nor did I want to spend a lot), which was why I hired our old college friend.

Bad choice.

And a bad idea to suggest that he represent both of us.

Right after we drafted what looked like a balanced and reasonable settlement, the lawyer advised her to take it to another attorney; he said he didn't want to be in a conflict-of-interest situation (translation: he didn't want to be sued for malpractice), which he could've been accused of since he was technically *my* attorney.

Needless to say, once I heard that I should've scrapped the whole plan and gone back to square one. But I was naïve. I assumed that my wife wanted to make this whole nightmare go away as much and as quickly as I did, and that she would simply pass it by another attorney for a fast rubber stamping.

Dumb!

To my surprise, my wife hired one of the best divorce lawyers in the county. But instead of then finding my own champion gunslinger, I stuck with my old buddy out of loyalty (amazing to think that I was more loyal to him than I was to my wife). I know; I was a chump.

As you know by now, her attorney used our negotiated document as the starting point for a whole new set of negotiations. They wiped the floor with me.

Moral: Don't try to save money on the attorney. It'll cost you more in the long run, and could end up hurting you for the rest of your life.

To begin the attorney-selection process, ask people you know who've been divorced for recommendations. Then ask everyone you know if they've ever heard of a good divorce lawyer, whether or not they're divorced. Ask your accountant, broker, banker, and doctor (who's probably been divorced more than once). The more people you ask, the better. That'll allow you to hear whether certain names keep popping up.

Once you've identified your top three, schedule confidential consultations with each. Even if it costs you a few hundred bucks per meeting, it's worth it for what you'll learn. Then, too, once you've actually handed them the money, that takes them out of the pool of attorneys your husband can use; an attorney who takes money from you can't represent anyone who opposes you. It's the law. So you benefit in two ways: You find the best attorney, and you keep your husband from hiring numbers two and three.

Here's what to keep in mind during that initial consult: This man or woman across the desk from you is going to be your primary confidant for some of the most emotionally trying days of your life, and possibly hold your future in his or her hands. Do you feel comfortable with that, relying on this person? Do you sense a connection between you, or the potential for a connection?

Here's what to ask and say at that meeting:

Tell me about your experience.

Where's your law degree from, and when did you get it?

How many years have you been practicing?

How many divorces do you handle a year? What's your current caseload?

What's your hourly rate and how do you bill — quarter-hour increments, or ten minutes at a time, or minute by minute?

How much is your required retainer?

Who in your office is going to do most of the work on this case, and how much does that person charge per hour?

What's your paralegal's rate?

Do you usually negotiate settlements or litigate, and what do you expect in this case?

Will I get itemized monthly bills?

What do you expect of me?

How accessible will you be to me when I call?

From what you've heard of my case so far, do you have a sense of what I might reasonably expect from a settlement and alimony and child support?

How long do you expect the whole process to take?

Do you know, or know of, my husband? If so, how?

How much malpractice insurance coverage do you carry?

Don't worry. It's not as grueling as it sounds. In the words of my old buddy, "Anticipation is worse than participation."

In selecting the attorney you like best or feel most confident with, never lose sight of the fact that this man or woman has to represent what's in *your* best interests. Really ugly divorces sometimes end up making only the lawyers rich, and that's something to be avoided, so make sure that this attorney isn't just an ego-mad gladiator who'd burn down the arena with you and everyone else in it just for the sake of winning.

All right, you've chosen your attorney. Now you have to play the role of employer. That means you have to manage your new employee. If you allow the lawyer to run wild, he will. Don't be afraid to advise him specifically what you want out of the divorce and what you're willing to give up. And never forget that every time you talk with him, and he talks to opposing counsel, someone is paying. Be prepared with a list of questions that need answering before you pick up the phone. If you make small talk about the weather, or can't find your questions, you'll be paying for wasted time. (Sometimes the judge requires the legal fees to be paid prior to asset distribution, so even though your husband is technically picking up the tab for your lawyer — probably, not certainly — you end up actually paying half of all the legal bills.)

That said, never forget that you hired the best attorney you could find — so take his advice! He's the pro. He's the one who's been there a thousand times before. He's the one who knows what's normal and abnormal. He knows what's reasonable and what's unreasonable.

By managing your attorney and taking his advice, you're halfway to a successful divorce. No, it's not going to be easy, and yes, you're going to be on an emotional elevator for a long time. But with the help of your attorney, some day the doors are going to open on a floor where you can buy freedom and happiness.

Chapter 7

HOW TO SURVIVE A DIVORCE

Regardless of the anger, hate, and hurt you may feel, trying some of the following strategies can minimize the long-term effects of an ugly divorce. However, to implement any of them, you'll have to control your emotions and not let them control you.

1. Establish the rules upfront. No one knows better than I how hard it is to have a civil, courteous conversation with the person you're trying to slaughter in divorce court. But it's absolutely essential that you establish, or at least try to, some acceptable rules of engagement. Examples: Agree not to drop in on the other person unannounced, even if you're just there to see the kids. Agree not to call each other, no matter how angry or vengeful you feel, before and after certain hours. Agree not to remove any personal property from the house until its final disposition is determined by the courts. And most importantly, agree on a blood oath not to talk to the kids about how bad the other person is. Keeping to these agreements can alleviate some of the most painful fighting that divorces tend to engender.

It might help you — both of you, actually — to think of the divorce as a boxing match. The combatants don't fight until they're in the ring (well, they're not supposed to), then, after the bell sounds they pound on each other until the bell goes off again. At the final bell, they hug. If it works for boxing, I think it could work for divorcing combatants. It's just too bad we don't have referees in real life handing out fouls and deducting points for hitting below the belt.

2. Try to keep the important negotiating for the attorneys. The reason you've hired an attorney to represent you is not only because he knows the law and parameters better than you, but because he can do what needs to be done objectively, without inserting emotion — and you can't. That means you can't let your soon-to-be ex suck you directly into discussions or arguments about who's going to get what. Whenever he tries — and he will — just tell him to talk it over with your attorney. Do not, under any circumstances, negotiate or discuss without your attorney being present. Not only will you be assured of getting the best possible settlement, you'll also have the satisfaction of knowing that you've driven him stark raving mad with frustration; the attorneys and court will be telling him when and what he can and can't do. Stand back and enjoy the sight of his rants. These days, they're likely to be better than most Hollywood movies.

3. Manage your attorney. Yes, we've been over this ground before, in the last chapter. But it can't hurt to re-emphasize that he gets paid by the hour. Unless he's the most scrupulous lawyer in town (talk about damning with faint praise), he doesn't benefit all that much if the divorce gets settled too quickly. What he could conceivably do is advise you to demand more than is reasonable, just to keep the game going. Or he may suggest that you refuse a reasonable counter offer, for the same reason.

Bottom line: Your job is to remain vigilant and cognizant.

4. Expect emotional highs and lows, and try to manage them. I'm told that some of the best sex couples ever have is when they're going through a divorce. Why not? You have all the ingredients for an operatic kind of passion — more passion, frankly, than most have ever felt. The danger, though, is that they'll misconstrue the sex as some sort of reconciliation.

By the same token, there will be days when you just want the divorce done now, no matter if you don't get what's just and right; you can't stand this protracted agony anymore.

In other words, your emotions are going through a washing machine, being bathed in hormones. Don't give in.

Don't weaken. Don't lose your way.

It might help you to keep in mind that you're not the first person to go through a divorce, and that everyone who has, has survived.

5. Manage your passion/anger. Thanks to that hormone/anger bath, you may just do something during the divorce process that will haunt you, or cause you pain, for the rest of your life. Be on guard against it. Don't be tempted to decide that, if you can't have your husband, no one can — which is what more than one woman has done in the past. (Men, too, actually.)

My best advice on this is to seek psychological counseling immediately if you feel yourself drowning in anger or depression or both. A pro can help you regain your perspective and self-esteem, and deal with the emotional turbulence. If necessary, he can prescribe any medications you might need, whether it's for help in sleeping or to alleviate depression. The good news is that your husband will have to pick up the tab.

6. Keep family and friends out of it. Or try to. Believe me, it's going to be difficult to confine the tumult between you, your lawyer, your doctor, your therapist, and your husband. But you have to try, for the sake of all the rest of your relationships. If necessary, include a close and trusted friend in the mix, and keep everyone else away. I have a friend who is now going through a very ugly divorce. His soon to be ex-wife is being advised by eight very angry women who have been hurt so badly by past relationships that they're out to castrate every male they come into contact with. Every time his ex spends time with "the committee of eight", she gets crazier and crazier. Unfortunately, his marriage is one of those that really should be made to work and could respond favorably to counseling if she would only keep the others out of their business. They are perfect for each other. And, talking to anyone who will listen makes it nearly impossible to minimize the amount and intensity of emotion you experience. And trying to turn everyone against your husband makes it impossible down the line to reconcile or have a civil relationship during the post-divorce period.

I remember when my ex sent a letter to everyone we knew, telling them about what an evil person I was and listing a zillion bad things I'd done to her. I'm sure writing it made her feel better for a while, but only for a while; soon enough she realized how silly it made her look, and noticed how unnecessarily she'd pissed me off. In the long run, she gained nothing. As the aphorism goes: Mud slung is ground lost.

7. Try to be reasonable in dividing property.
Walking with a friend through a flea market in Miami, I asked a vendor how much some little child's knickknack was; I wanted to buy it for one of my daughters, and figured it cost a buck or two. "Two hundred dollars," he said. "What?" I shrieked. "Sure," he said, "it's an antique."

Pretty much the same thing happens with the division

of property. Suddenly that thing you forgot to throw out eight years ago is now, with the spotlight on it, worth seven figures. It's not so much that you or he really wants it; it's that neither of you wants the other to get it.

In my long and invaluable experience dividing assets after a marriage gone sour, I've found that the most efficient method is to begin by making a list of all property to be divided. You hand copies to both parties, and then have each check off which items they want and feel entitled to. When that's done, the lists are exchanged — and the parties separate for the night, each to go over the other's list alone, in private, calmly.

Then, the next day, they give a revised copy of their demands to their respective attorneys. A dollar value is then assigned to the disputed items before the negotiations begin. Believe it or not, this process actually takes a lot of the anger and fighting out of this phase of the process, and generally results in a fairer division of property. When my second ex and I did this, we both ended up wanting a unique piece of art that had been in the house. Independently of each other, we valued the sculpting, and then had the choice of taking it or getting the equivalent in cash without a big fight. I chose the cash. Given the size of the settlement check I was going to have to write, I needed the $7,500 more than I needed art. We both felt like we won!

8. What to seek in a divorce. Divorce laws vary from state to state, so settlements necessarily vary state to state. I noted some of the variables earlier, such as whether there are children in the home and how old they are. It's your lawyer's job to give you a comprehensive list of what you can expect. Even so, there are some things that can get overlooked or downplayed during the process, possibly because they seem irrelevant or inconsequential at the time.

Pension, 401K, IRA, or Social Security benefits. You may be entitled to share in these benefits or share in a portion of those assets in the future.

Collectibles. If one spouse owns a large, valuable collection of art, coins, cars, baseball cards, or anything that may be viewed as a material asset, you might be able to get the cash value of half that asset.

Frequent flyer miles. It sounds silly, I know, but some men have accumulated a treasure chest's worth of free plane trips or free hotel nights. You might be entitled to share them with him.

Money for the kids' education, all the way from pre-school to grad school. Be sure that when college expenses are identified in the settlement agreement that tuition, room, board, books, activities fees, and transportation to and from school are also included. Also, try to minimize the amount of decision-making authority your ex has with regard to the college's selection. I remember when a friend's daughter was accepted to Columbia, but the ex used the veto power he'd gained in the agreement and refused to pay the high tuition. The poor girl ended up enrolling in a state school — and hating her father. He didn't care.

Money for the kids' extracurricular activities, like sports

and dance and swimming lessons, cheerleading, gymnastics, tutoring, and music. Add them all up over a period of years, and you're talking some serious money that you'd either have to fight over or split, or both, if you don't outline the costs in the divorce agreement.

In the event you or the ex moves away, go for reimbursement of long-distance calls and travel expenses associated with visitation.

If you're not working at the time the divorce comes through, you might be able to get him to pay the costs of getting you retrained and ready for the marketplace. Child support comes to you tax free, but alimony is considered taxable income; you'll have to either get a job to pay the taxes, or put some of that money away. So try to have more of the monthly support payment allocated as child support rather than alimony. Also, alimony ends if you remarry. Try not to have a "co-habitation" clause in your divorce agreement. This way you could live with someone and still get alimony.

Medical, dental, vision, and orthodontia are all costs that should be covered in the settlement — and paid by him. Also, try to include psychological counseling, in the event your child needs some help after the trauma of his parents' split.

Life insurance. Require your ex to maintain a policy naming your child (children) as beneficiary (beneficiaries).

Try also to get half of your husband's future bonuses and raises. This is doable if he rose up the corporate ladder while you were supporting him at home. And don't forget to get half of any stock options he may have/get.

Go for access to all of his future tax returns. This will allow you to determine whether he had a significant pay increase, which could require him to pay more in child support.

Try to get your children named on your own tax return as dependents. This could save you a ton in income taxes. At worst, you should be able to alternate years or each of you takes a child if you have two. (Make sure you take the youngest child as your dependent, you'll get the tax deduction longer!)

If you're so inclined, go for a requirement that he provide your children with cars and insurance when they turn driving age. That will allow them to get jobs and reduce your chauffeuring responsibilities.

Bottom line: You owe it to yourself and your family to be as *unreasonable* as you can in fighting for your rights. Let the attorney and the courts advise you when you've overstepped your bounds. You don't get what you're worth in this life; you get what you negotiate. And, if you don't ask, the answer is always NO!

Chapter 8

DIVORCE CAN MAKE
YOU CRAZY

Remember the movie *Fatal Attraction*, about the man who has what he thinks is a quick, no-obligation affair, only to find when he tries to dump her that he's got a psychotic on his hands? Well, more or less that describes what can happen when only one partner wants out of a marriage.

Let's say your husband comes home one day and demands a divorce, and you find out there's another woman involved. It's certainly not unlikely that you'd want to take the nearest lamp and smash it in his face, then wrap the cord around his neck and strangle him slowly, his last words a plea for his life. *Fat chance, buster.*

Yes, women can do — or fantasize doing — irrational and crazy things when going through a divorce. But if you don't want to spend the next zillion years is prison, like the Texas woman who ran over her husband three times after finding out he was having an affair, then you need to control yourself — with a straitjacket, if necessary. No matter how good even small acts of revenge and rage may feel at the moment, you'll definitely want to avoid the following:

1. Destroying personal property. It stands to reason that if you want to get back at me, you're not going to burn down my neighbor's house. Likewise, you're going to want to get back at your lying, pond-scum husband not by taking out your hostilities on your own possessions, but on something that he particularly values. On this, I speak from experience.

I remember coming back from a business trip and finding a sledgehammer in my office. I asked my secretary what it was doing there, and she said my wife had dropped it off. Apparently my wife was convinced I was having an affair and wasn't really out of town on a business trip. She'd been driving around all night, cruising the parking lots of the city's hotels, looking for my car — ready to turn it into scrap.

Then there's the story of when my friend's wife who took an X-acto knife to the sleeves of his Armani suits. And the one about the wife of a contractor I know who had a company employee fill her husband's classic Corvette convertible with cement. The stories never end.

The point here is that whatever jollies such acts of vandalism give you, they're going to be short-lived…and long regretted. Besides prejudicing the judge against you (something you want to avoid at all costs), they could conceivably get a jury to convict you. Believe me, the courts don't have a sense of humor. And if you have kids, don't expect custody.

Bottom line: One way or another, you're going to pay for that moment of fun.

2. Initiate some form of personal abuse to replicate physical abuse. If you read the newspapers regularly, you've undoubtedly seen stories of women who purposely hurt themselves in order either to get sympathy from their husbands as a way of keeping them from leaving, or to increase their leverage in settlement negotiations. This is, as you'll undoubtedly agree, an act of colossal stupidity and wrong-headedness. Additionally, fraud and submitting false police reports are crimes that could end your butt in jail.

One of my wives would sometimes get right up in my face and spit and scream and spew the vilest obscenities and insults, all in an attempt to provoke me into hitting her; that, she thought, would put her in the driver's seat for all negotiations. When it didn't work (I kept my hands in my pockets and then walked away), she tried slapping herself and throwing herself down on the floor, falling from the lower steps, to make it appear that I really had lashed out. Then she'd call the police while crying hysterically, accusing me of using her as a punching bag. Twice the police showed up and immediately recognized that this was an irrational basket case whose testimony couldn't possibly be believed; they knew that the marks on her body were self-inflicted.

When we finally settled, it turned out that her own irrationality hurt her. After reading the police report, the judge was more sympathetic to me than he might've been.

Bottom line: Don't do it.

3. Try to embarrass him. I mentioned earlier how one of my wives tried to get vengeance on me by smearing my name to everyone and anyone; it was a campaign, as I noted, that backfired on her when people began whispering that she'd *lost it.*

Beyond that though, there were more unintended consequences to her vicious crusade. One, she pissed me off so badly that she killed any chance we might have had to reconcile; two, by trying to damage my career and earning power, she was inadvertently damaging her settlement potential.

Here's something to keep in mind: When you're going through a divorce, no one really cares about your problems; they have problems of their own. To this day, friends still laugh derisively about the crazy Christmas letters my ex-wife wrote about our relationship that had, by then, been long over.

As Lincoln said, "Tis better to keep silent and be thought a fool than to open your mouth and erase all doubt." Don't make yourself the punch line of a bad joke.

4. "The New You." You know what that means,

right? It's when the woman decides to take on a new persona — change her hair, wear short skirts, date bikers 15 years her junior, get a tattoo and nose ring and belly ring at 40.

Well, you know what? It doesn't work. As with my wife who tried to make herself bigger by making me smaller, people generally laugh behind your back. Human misery, unfortunately, is the best show in town for most people. They slow down and gawk at it as though it were car accident. Don't be one. Don't give up either your common sense or your self-respect. Stay true to who you are, no matter how mad or hurt or angry you are. At least those are authentic emotions — unlike that new image.

5. Go out with, or have sex with, one of your ex-husband's friends. Inexplicably, this phenomenon happens often enough to almost be a cliché. It's a form of vengeance, I suppose, but a uniquely ugly form of it.

The woman going through a hurtful divorce wants her husband to feel the pain she felt, and figures that the best way to inflict it is by dating or having sex with someone close to him, just to provoke his feelings of jealousy and hurt.

There are many problems with this approach, not least of which is that the woman generally hurts herself as much as she hurts both her husband and her husband's friendship. She ends up being used and, once again, only looks foolish; she's become a walking cliché, pathetic and pitiable. You know why? Because her husband already knows that if the guy she's dating was really his friend, he wouldn't have gone out with her in the first place.

Here's hoping that the crazy behaviors identified in this chapter will help you to accept that "*feeling crazy*" at this time is normal, but that *acting it out* is likely to hurt you most of all.

Bottom line: The best revenge for a cheating husband is a great settlement, and then living well off it.

Chapter 9

KIDS BEFORE, DURING
AND AFTER

Under the best of circumstances (whatever those may be), getting divorced is amazingly stressful. But it's geometrically worse when the two of you have kids. Not only are you forced to deal with all of the emotions of losing your significant other, but you then have to add in your guilt and concern over the impact the divorce is going to have on your kids.

If your soon-to-be ex is any kind of father, he'll be going through the same conflicting emotions — but don't think for a moment that he won't try to use your maternal instincts to his advantage during and after settlement negotiations.

What follows isn't an extensive case study of everything that can and might happen when kids are involved; it's a short list of the three most significant potential problems to keep in mind and watch for.

1. **Troubled kids.** Seeing parents go through a divorce — and feeling the tension in the home caused by it — can turn the world's best kid into the bad seed.

Kids deal with their emotions in different ways, depending on their age. Teens, for example, sometimes let their grades drop; or they may start acting up and get in trouble — fighting, taking drugs, drinking alcohol, smoking cigarettes.

One thing to watch for is whether they start hanging out with a bad group of kids. Or whether they quit their sports teams or clubs. What they're trying to do is send you a signal that they're hurting and need your attention. Subconsciously, maybe even consciously, they're thinking that if they become a problem, then Dad and Mom will have to get back together and solve it. Be sensitive to them and dote as much as possible. Take them to seek help. Remember above all that how you handle them could have lifelong implications for their well-being and health.

Younger children tend to act out more directly. They might suddenly turn mean and start hitting, or do damage to your house. Most child shrinks will tell you that this is their way of showing you their anger and hurt; they're screaming for help. Your job is to watch for the signs and answer their call.

As with teens, I strongly recommend that you get your young children some counseling both during and after the divorce. Talking to a professional who's "seen it all" before will help them to keep things in perspective and understand that, contrary to what they may be feeling, the divorce is not their fault — and that life *will* go on.

2. Games kids play. Kids are little evil geniuses. Instinctively, they know your hot buttons; they know how to manipulate you to get what they want. Add to that the guilt that parents feel over the divorce, and some kids figure out how to get themselves new games, clothes, bikes, toys, computers, bigger allowances, extended curfews, even cars — you name it.

My response to this: It's a big friggin' mistake to give in to their emotional extortion!

Believe me, you cannot possibly buy your way out of your children's upset and turmoil over your divorce. No amount of PlayStation2's can make up for what they're losing, and giving them these things is actually harmful; they'll come to expect gifts every time they feel bad, which of course isn't exactly a strong basis for emotional health or maturity. Besides that, they'll actually resent you for giving in to what they know, in their evil genius, is wrong. Better that you give them what parents are supposed to give them: consistency, a structured environment, and discipline. Those will make them feel loved, which is exactly what they need.

After the divorce, if you have an argument with them that causes them to shout in anger, "Fine, I'll just go live with Dad," immediately get up and pack their bags. In other words, call their bluff. I can pretty much promise you that their urge to leave will pass quickly. Just please don't fold and give in to their demands. If you do, they'll pull this one on you forever.

3. Kids and the next relationship. Ah, dating. It's hard enough to do it when you're 18 and fancy-free. It's harder still to do it when you're just getting back in the saddle after a long and bumpy ride with some other cowboy. But it's hardest of all when Tex comes to your door and your kids say, "Go away, you're not my dad."

You can count on seeing some pretty miserable behavior from the little tots as they see you trying to enjoy your life again. Everything from being nasty to the new guy, to screaming like a little banshee in front of him, to trying to scare him off with snakes is more or less par for the course.

Myself, I remember Mom trying to date again a year or so after she and Dad divorced. I was 14 at the time, and she brought home this guy who actually slept on our downstairs sofa one night because he was too tired to drive home. When he woke in the morning, I stood over him holding a kitchen knife. "I don't want to see you here again," I said. And I didn't. Obviously, Mom was not very happy with me.

The point is that, no matter how rancorous or ugly the divorce process was, kids always hold out hope that their parents will get back together again. So when they see one parent happily involved in another relationship, they know the chances of that happening go way, way down.

Your job is to explain to them, calmly and rationally,

that you and their father can never be husband and wife again. Tell them also that they are the most important things in your life, but that you do indeed have a life, and you'd like to enjoy it, just like you hope that they will enjoy their lives. Divorce is a terrible thing, but it's not the death penalty.

I admit that I'm acutely sensitive to this particular aspect of the divorce story, given my experience. My three daughters from my first marriage became very close to their stepmother — my second wife. So when I divorced her, too, two of my daughters angrily did everything they could to hurt me and make me return to her. Since then they've flatly refused to acknowledge my new companion — or me, for that matter; they haven't spoken to me going on three years, and my oldest daughter didn't even invite me to her med school graduation or her wedding! It hurts, not least because they're adults who don't seem to understand an adult's choices and I thought I brought them up better than that. Someday, though, I hope, they'll come to understand how much they've missed by not keeping me in their lives. Until then, I live with that hope, and do my best not to let their choices destroy me. I must live my own life, just as you need to live yours.

Anyway, life is messy. Our job is to clean up the mess as best we can, and then accommodate the rest.

Chapter 10

LIFE AFTER DIVORCE

The oldest cliché in the book is no less true for being old: Time heals all wounds. (It also wounds all heels.) Which means, yes, that someday you'll feel like yourself again.

How do I know this? Because almost everything you feel; almost everything you'll go through; almost every event and issue that occur before, during, and after a divorce are virtually identical for almost everyone. True, you may be one of the lucky few that suffers little; if so, more power to you. This section, then, is for the vast majority who are likely to feel overwhelmed by what's happened to them. I want you to know that you're not the first person to feel this way, and I can only hope that you'll take some comfort in that. Forewarned, after all, is forearmed.

1. The check never comes on time. In other words,

"it's in the mail." Actually, it's in the *male*.

Men are used to having most of the power and control in the relationship. But now that the courts have decided *for him* what he has to pay out and when he can and can't see his kids, he feels helpless. He's lost his power over you. Or has he?

In his mind, consciously or subconsciously, he's got one little game to play in which he can declare himself the winner. That's right, the monthly check. Not sending it when he's supposed to, even while flirting with a possible contempt of court penalty, gives him the feeling that he's won: he has something you need — nananananana.

My advice, strongly urged, is to not get sucked into arguments about the monthly check. That only gives him what he wants, which is the satisfaction of knowing he's getting under your skin. Instead of saying something to him, the first time the check is late or isn't written for the full amount or isn't signed, have your attorney send him a letter advising him that he will be prosecuted for failure to comply with a court order and he will be responsible for all of your legal fees.

This will help you in two ways: First, he'll come to understand that he can only lose by playing games with monthly support checks; and two, you'll get the satisfaction of knowing that he's going crazy — he can't get the reaction from you that he wanted.

2. Continuous emotional power/control fights, especially if kids are involved. Think of this post-divorce period as an emotional roller coaster period for both of you. You're experiencing all of the emotions of being single again, and all of the anger and resentment of being single after vowing to stay together forever — and it's his fault, dammit.

Of course, he feels exactly the same — except that from his point of view, it's *your* fault. And you have *his* money.

Accordingly, the less contact you guys have with each other during this period, the better for both of you. As noted earlier, you're not going to be friends, and you're almost certainly not going to reconcile. What you'd do better to concentrate on is your own happiness and future. Naturally, though, if you have kids together, you're stuck with each other forever, or at least until one of you die.

With my first divorce, I needed to have ongoing contact with my ex, because I was either picking up the girls or calling to talk to them — and every visit was a constant reminder of how much I didn't like her. It was horrible in a thousand little ways. But with my second divorce, it was relatively painless, in that we hadn't had any children together. The absence of post-divorce contact minimized the stress for both of us.

3. Use kids as a lobbying force. One of the ugliest parts about divorce is how men frequently turn their kids into little messengers of doom, getting them to tell their mother about the financial trouble he's in. Meanwhile, the woman often turns them into Avon ladies, getting them to solicit their own desires. I remember how my kids would show up for the weekend with badly worn shoes or ratty clothes. This was my ex's way of forcing me to take them shopping, even though she was supposed to use her support money to buy those things.

I was no better, however. I'd lobby the kids for things I wanted, too.

Bottom line: Keep the kids out of it. Think of the biblical story about Solomon who had to decide which of two women was the real mother of an infant. When they both claimed the child as their own, he threatened to cut the child in two, giving half to each. It was the real mother who shouted no; she'd rather live without the child than see it harmed. That should be your attitude, too. Do what's best for your children, not for you.

4. Lifestyle changes dramatically. The house, a car, monthly cash — no matter what you end up with in the settlement, it's not going to be enough to make up for what you lost. Because what you lost is more than just financial; it's also emotional and physical and psychological; it's having to see your kids in pain; it's feeling lonely and depressed; it's experiencing failure. Money and houses and cars can't make up for that.

But even if they could, you'll probably find that being chief cook and bottle washer has left you with a lot less than you thought you were getting. Most likely, you'll have to tighten your belt a bit. Vacations will be different, probably not so lavish. The food you buy and prepare at home won't be quite as fancy. You'll go out to eat less, and eat more at less expensive places. And you'll almost certainly wait for sales before you go shopping for shoes and clothes.

Bottom line: It's a big adjustment. Prepare yourself.

5. "In retrospect, the past wasn't so bad." This is called post-divorce remorse. And it's as natural as gravity.

Most people tend to see the past through rose-colored glasses. The farther in the past something is, the more likely they are to put a rosy tint on it. In fact, rubbing the hard edges off of bad memories can keep us going every day and give us hope.

Add to that tendency the pain you're probably experiencing in the present, and suddenly the past seems like a Disney movie. "What ugly stuff?" you'll ask yourself.

And when you do, you'll be particularly vulnerable to the desire to patch things up with your ex and try to get back together. A surprisingly large number of people actually do give in to this temptation, and it's not so surprising when they discover, all over again, why they got divorced in the first place.

Example: My female friend who, like Liz Taylor and Richard Burton, married and divorced the same person twice. She married him the second time, she said, because she "was so miserable when they were divorced, it was almost like they were married." (The songwriter Steven Bishop once said, "I'm so miserable without you, it's almost like having you here.")

Bottom line: If it didn't work out the first time, it's probably not going to work out the second time, either. Don't give in to the remorse. The only way out to the other side is through the pain. Stick with it and know that it's going to get better.

6. Exercise to manage stress. Stress is a certified killer, and divorce is a certified creator of stress, which by the transitive property means that divorce can be a killer. Don't let it happen.

Some people manage stress by drinking alcohol and taking drugs. But that's like breaking a window to get some fresh air. A far better and healthier way to manage stress is through exercise. Exercise gets your blood circulating and oxygenated, and it releases the body's natural opiates, endorphins, into the bloodstream. The results, if you're not already an exerciser, will surprise you. You'll feel better, sleep better, look better, and improve your energy, your outlook, your self-esteem — and your chances of meeting someone new.

Not so incidentally, there's no better feeling than to look utterly fabulous when your ex comes to pick up the kids. It'll eat him up, I promise. A friend of mine who'd abandoned his wife of 14 years for his girlfriend, leaving his wife devastated, ran into her on the street about six months later. She'd spent those six months working out, and boy, did she look great. That afternoon, he began begging her to let him come back, and he's been begging ever since. As she learned, the best revenge is not only to live well, but to look good.

7. Avoid blind dates, and have lunch, coffee, or

drinks instead of dinners when you do date. In general, blind dates are a step above going to a funeral, but a *bad* blind date makes you wish you were the one in the coffin.

Your friends, no doubt, mean well when they insist on setting you up "with this terrific guy." When they suggest this, step back, make the sign of the cross, and put a string of garlic around your neck. But if that doesn't work, and they still insist, arrange the meeting so that it's more informal and casual — say, at a cocktail party, or with a large group of people, where each of you can size up the other without all the one-on-one pressure. And if you can't arrange that, then turn the date into lunch, or coffee, or an after-work drink. All three of those carry far fewer expectations, and are finished sooner, than an evening out. If, by chance, you do hit it off, you can make immediate plans to get together soon — that night, even.

A word of warning, though: Go slowly. Not only are you emotionally confused and fragile, you certainly don't want to appear desperate, which is what men often infer from aggressive, hungry, recently divorced women.

8. Meet new men in places other than bars. Have you ever known a steady couple that met each other in a bar? Neither have I. The bar scenes suck (That's why they're called meat markets). They're filled with desperate singles looking to hook up but lacking the resources, initiative, and creativity to find alternative means.

There are plenty of alternatives to bars if you're interested in meeting men. Your church or synagogue is a good start. So is your health club, your country club, your neighborhood, your kids' schools, sporting events, grocery stores, malls, parties, professional groups, university extension courses or school in general, and alumni clubs, to name only a few.

Then, too, don't be shy about letting people know that you're out there again; and don't forget that we tend to find what we're looking for when we're *not* looking for it. The more pressure you put on yourself to find someone, the less likely you are to do so. Men can smell the desperation, and it's a turn-off to them. That doesn't mean, however, that you shouldn't make eye contact and smile — the best ways to let men know you're available. You most definitely should. A smile tells men that it's okay to approach you, that you won't bite them.

Example: A really wonderful female friend of mine used to stop herself from smiling because she felt self-conscious about her teeth. One day I asked her which was worse, being alone or risking someone not liking her teeth? At last she got the courage to smile at men she liked — and guess what? She met a dentist, they fell in love, and he fixed her teeth.

Another interesting way to meet people is on the Internet; in fact, millions are out there right now, hooking up with each other. But you have to be incredibly careful and cautious. Here you are, sharing your most personal feelings with someone whom you know not at all. He may or may not even be a he, and he may or may not be married, and he may or may not be a lawyer from Waukegan. So don't rush to give out your personal contact information, like home phone and address. If you want to arrange a meeting, do it in a place where people know you, and you know you'll be safe. If, when he walks in, he's not as he described himself — say, he's short, fat, and bald, when he claimed to be tall and thin with wavy hair — walk out immediately; if he's lied about that, he's likely lied about other things, too.

My advice is to join one of several reputable Internet dating services, such as Match.com, which does a great job getting people together. The participants post a photo, a brief essay about their likes and dislikes, a profile of their ideal date and partner, and a preferred geographical radius from which to select the other. Potential match-ups are then given means to exchange email addresses. From there, it's up to you.

Personally, I think this is a great way to meet people, particularly for older people who wouldn't anyway feel comfortable hanging out in bars or health clubs.

9. Personal ads: If you really want to humiliate yourself, run an ad or respond to a personal ad in the newspaper. What are these people thinking when they do that? But before you do, let's try to think about this objectively, logically, and unemotionally.

First of all, if you're going to post an ad, what are you going to say about yourself? "Divorced woman who is biter, out of shape, low on cash, with three neurotic kids, looking for her Mr. Right to ease her pain"? I don't think so. You're going to highlight, and possibly even embellish a little, every quality you have, and probably avoid going into any of the potential negatives. In the ad, you may not even mention the fact that you're a single mom. So, if this is the case with you, what makes you think that the other postings are any different?

In fact, if you want to have some fun, grab a glass of wine and read some of those personal ads with a friend, they really can be quite entertaining. If a person has to say he's "smart", he's probably not, and very insecure about it. If someone says he's "looking for a woman to share poetry or long romantic walks on the beach", he's probably wresting with his own sexuality or will say just about anything to get into your pants.

Or how about the one "looking for a companion for life"....*really*, in the want ads? You need to look at personal ads a lot the same way you look at real estate ads. Just as a "fixer upper" is another way of calling it a money pit, "Mr. tall, dark and handsome" is probably only 5'3" with a face that only a mother could love. Consider yourself forewarned. Don't waste your time or money chasing Mr. Right in the personal ads. When you finally meet him, you'll probably discover he's Mr. Wrong, or Mr. Turn N. Run.

However, the best personal ad story I've ever heard was about an ad that was run in "The Atlanta Journal" and was reported to have received thousands of responses. You may have seen it before because it was heavily circulated on the Internet. The ad read: "SINGLE BLACK FEMALE...Seeks male companionship, ethnicity unimportant. I'm a very good-looking female who LOVES to play. I love long walks in the woods, riding in your pickup truck, hunting, camping, fishing trips, and cozy winter nights lying by the fire. Candlelight dinners will have me eating out of your hand. Rub me the right way, and watch me respond. I'll be there at the front door when you get home from work, wearing only what nature gave me. Kiss me and I'm yours. Call xxx-xxx and ask for Daisy."

In response to this ad, over 15,000 men found themselves talking to the local Humane Society about an 8-week old, black female Labrador retriever named Daisy. Point made? Things may not always be what they seem in personal ads; be careful, or better yet, don't bother!

10. Forgive, forget, and move on. After all the polluted emotional water that rushed under your marital bridge, the hardest thing to do now is just to let go of the past and move on. If you don't, you'll be stuck forever — like one of my ex-wives was with me. She kept reminding herself of my indiscretions, of how much she'd loved me and how much I'd hurt her; and she kept calling me with invitations to go on trips with her, and to help her make certain decisions. This went on for almost two years after the divorce. I begged her to stop, but she wouldn't until her therapist got her to realize that it wasn't meant to be between us, and that she had to forgive, forget, and move on if she was ever going to get well. Finally, she did. If only she'd understood earlier that I, like most ex-husbands, kind of got off on her neediness, and in fact it would've made me absolutely crazy if she'd just been able to turn and walk away. What a weapon against me that would've been — a spear right through my ego. Don't forget that.

11. Comparing new people to your old spouse.

There is a tendency after divorce, especially among women who married early and were married a long time, to compare every new man in their life to their ex-husbands. It's only natural, I suppose, since their husbands were their major reference points about the male of the species. But arsenic is natural, too.

A dear female friend was married for 15 years to an alpha male kind of guy — dominant and yet personable. Recently she met a man she refers to as her "new love", but right away talks about him (when he's not there) as lacking her ex-husband's personality and gregariousness. Uh-oh. She can't on the one hand claim to love the new guy and at the same time compare him to an imaginary yardstick — especially one that's been elongated and sanded by her rose-colored memories. In her mind, her husband has now become even more charming, more attractive, more captivating than she experienced him back then. And it's going to be as much of a problem for her in the future as it is for young women who idealize their fathers.

Even today, when one of my ex-wives tells me how Mr. So and So is much nicer and sweeter and better and whatever than I am, I know that what she's really saying is that she still has *me* under her skin. That's not the message, I'm sure, you want to send to your ex, either.

12. Get professional advice to manage your finances and investments. If your husband managed all of your investments and monthly bills, you will undoubtedly be at a serious disadvantage having to suddenly be responsible for everything pertaining to money. I remember when my ex wife shrunk the nest egg she'd been given in the divorce settlement by over 30 percent in the first four months. It wasn't her fault, except to the degree that she refused to take professional advice, because she'd never had to do things like that before. Don't make the same mistake.

A good financial planner is a necessity if your settlement amounts to anything substantial (or frankly, even if it doesn't). Asking for advice is nothing to be ashamed of. Even the big guys, with seven-figure incomes and nine-figure net worth, rely on finance professionals. So should you. Don't let the fees they charge stop you from hiring them. In the long run, it'll be one of the best investments you ever make.

13. Alcohol consumption. We've seen it in movies and plays, and read it in books for as long as movies and plays and books have been written — the depressed man or woman drowning his or her sorrows in alcohol. Depressed? "Whiskey, Sal, and make it a double."

Well, alcohol frequently plays a big role in divorces, given the amount of emotional pain that the partners would just as soon numb themselves from experiencing. I won't, here, give you my pep talk about how alcohol never solved anything, and blah blah blah. Instead, I'll simply point out that alcohol is a depressant, which is hardly what you need when you're depressed — like giving a glass of water to a drowning man.

Alcohol will only exaggerate your mood swings and make you less likely to sort out what you're really feeling from what the alcohol adds. Besides, getting drunk increases the likelihood of making truly terrible decisions, decisions you don't even known you're making. Drunken people attract each other, and people who get drunk aren't people you want attracted to you.

Then there's the matter of DUI. On her way home from a bar, the police stopped a friend of mine, who began drinking during her divorce proceedings. She claimed she'd only had a drink or two and was perfectly fine, but her weaving had told them a different story. She ended up spending several hours in jail, losing her license for a year, and wasting thousands of dollars on legal fees. Now she has to ride her bicycle to the grocery store, which as you can imagine makes getting on with life a lot more difficult. Luckily for her, though, she doesn't have any kids. If she did, the DUI conviction would have almost certainly jeopardize her child custody. How, after all, can she do what needs to be done with her children when she can't even drive?

Bottom line: You're vulnerable, and as much as you want to drink to feel less vulnerable, it won't work. And, it could negatively impact you for a long time, if not the rest of your life.

14. Get a pet. I'm not kidding about this. It's a great idea. Even if you already have a pet or pets, a new puppy or kitty in the house gives you something new on which to re-focus your volatile emotions, and does it in a healthy, constructive way. In fact, getting a new pet could be salutary for the entire family for the same reasons that old people who are given animals tend to live longer and with fewer complaints about their own ailments.

Personally, I prefer dogs; they're far more affectionate and demonstrative than cats, which is exactly what you need right now. Imagine a little puppy, with all its joyful energy and unconditional love running around your house or taking you for walks. Incidentally, dogs are probably the best way to meet new people. Who, after all, can resist petting a little pup and then asking you about him? If nothing else, the little guy will help you get your mind off yourself and onto something that's absolutely life-affirming. And for those who can't stand the thought of housebreaking, there are always animal rescue centers that have great dogs who've already been trained, fixed, and inoculated; they're just looking for a good home. Like yours.

One last note: Providing a good home for a pet means having a good home for yourself, too.

Chapter 11

THE NEXT RELATIONSHIP

All right, you've survived your divorce and are ready (or at least willing) to get on with your life. The question is: How can you succeed in your next relationship?

The answer: Learn from your past mistakes. In the words of the great philosopher George Santayana, "Those who cannot, or will not, remember the past are condemned to repeat it." So here are a few things you should've learned before moving on.

1. Become comfortable with being alone. The best — and in fact the only — way to truly enjoy the company of others is to enjoy being alone with yourself first. The explanation for this isn't difficult. Being comfortable by yourself reduces your neediness level, thus reducing the neuroses that you'll exhibit the moment you're not getting exactly what you want from your new partner. Instead of reacting in panic out of fear that your lifeline might be pulled away, you'll be able to stay in the moment with your partner (indeed, with anyone); you'll deal with the situation at hand, not fight old battles with your old husband (or even someone before him, which may, in fact, have been your problem with your husband).

Not needing someone else will also give you the patience to wait for the right person, rather than accepting the first warm body who says yes, as a friend of mine did after unexpectedly losing her husband. This man had been her whole life, and did everything for her. When he was gone and she had only herself, she felt she had nothing...so she quickly jumped into a new relationship. After only a few months together, she let him move in with her, but because he didn't like being in her first husband's house, they bought a new one together. Almost as soon as they closed escrow she realized that she'd been on the rebound this whole time. It took nearly a year, and a lot of emotional turmoil, to undo the handcuffs that could have been avoided if she'd only been more patient, which she would have been had she enjoyed her own company. Don't make the same mistake.

2. Form a support group of new friendships.

Barbara Streisand had it right 40 years ago: People need people. We need to share ourselves with others, and we need others to share themselves with us. Whether it's a good friend, a sister, a neighbor, we need at least one other person we can count on to be there for us — to give us confirmation and validation, and sometimes just to listen.

Not long ago I had the pleasure of attending a women's faith-based mentoring support group — ten women who met weekly to talk about whatever happened to be going on in their lives. What a wonderful experience it was to meet them, this collection of divorced, married, widowed, thinking of divorce, thinking of marrying, etc. women, all of whom (I quickly saw) had each other's best interests at heart. There was no competition between them, no pretense, no catty judging — just pure support. Every woman could speak freely, knowing that whatever was said in that room would stay in that room. It was an extraordinary and wonderful thing to behold, and got me thinking how necessary it is for everyone to have such a safe place to go, but especially those who've just recently gone through the trauma of divorce.

Groups like these are springing up all over the place, and can be found rather easily through your church, synagogue, or the Internet. But if, by chance, you can't find one in your area, why not start your own group? That is, after all, how every existing group came into being — by one person having the idea and making the first call.

3. Don't abandon your girlfriends every time a new man comes into your life.
When I was a kid, my mother used to recite a couplet that's endured through the ages for its wisdom: "Make new friends but keep the old, because one is silver, the other is gold." True words indeed, but never more

profoundly so than when it comes to your girlfriends not being replaced in your life by whatever pair of pants you happen to be dating at the moment. How can you reasonably expect to develop meaningful, intimate relationships with other women when you drop them at the first sign of new meat? Why should they invest the time and energy in you, knowing that they're only way stations?

I remember my ex-wife talking about one of her girlfriends who hung with her girlfriends only when she didn't have a man around. The minute she met him, she'd disappear for months. No calls, no lunches, no shopping, no coffee. Then, when the relationship ended (and it always did), she'd be back — complaining about the guy who'd just left her.

Don't let that be you.

4. Learn from your prior mistakes. To the degree that you can look back objectively — that is, without letting yourself off the hook too easily or being unduly hard on yourself — take the time to evaluate what went wrong in your marriage. Look at what you wanted and what you got, then at what you did to get what you wanted, and what you didn't do. Only you can take whatever corrective actions are necessary.

5. Move slowly and cautiously; it's not a race. There are no points awarded for she who lands him the fastest. Take your time and get to know him before you start solidifying the relationship. And for God's sake, don't just rush to jump into bed with him, particularly if you were married a long time; this first naked encounter is likely to feel uncomfortable — that is, unless you let it happen slowly and organically as an outgrowth of emotional affection, not physical lust. You'll know when it's time, and if he truly is the right man, he'll understand and be supportive of your caution.

6. Know if the man you meet is married. I'm sure I don't have to tell you that the last thing you want to do is get mixed up with a married man. First, if there was an "other woman" who helped break up your marriage, remember how you felt; you don't want to do the same to someone else. Secondly, you don't want to waste your time on a relationship with a man who, if by chance you do hit it off together, can't give himself to you completely. Third, involvement with a married man will slow your recovery from the pain of the past.

Unfortunately, men can be superb liars — and, through practice, have mastered the art of hiding the fact that they are indeed married. Which means it's up to *you* to verify their marital status. How you do that is up to you. But it's not hard at all if you really want to (emphasis on the "really"; a lot of women don't want to look too hard for fear of finding something they don't want to see).

Start by asking. Some men won't volunteer the truth, but they'll tell you if you ask.

Also, be wary of the "I'm separated" answer, which was the one I used to use way back when. It was technically the truth — sort of. There I was, hanging out in a bar, while my wife was home with the kids. Therefore, we were technically separated.

My other answer was, "I'm living with a married woman," which usually brought a hearty laugh, allowing me to quickly change the subject. I can't tell you the number of times I got away with either answer. It was obvious to me that a lot of women asked the question perfunctorily and then listened for any answer other than "yes." In other words, they heard what they wanted to hear.

Hint: One way he says "yes" without knowing it, is by having a tan line on his finger where his wedding ring resides…when he's not out on the prowl. Another is when he repeatedly apologizes for not being able to get together on weekends and weekend nights.

One almost sure-fire "yes" is his not allowing you to call him at home or only on his cell phone. Another is his reluctance to invite you to his home or office.

If he does invite you to his house, look to see what kinds of photos he has on display. See if the frames match the dust lines on the furniture, indicating that the real things may be hiding in the closet for the night, while presumably his wife is in Toledo visiting her folks. If that passes the smell test, check the medicine cabinet, which a man is likely to forget to clean out of feminine products. For instance, if you see a bottle of Midol, a tube of lipstick, and some Nair, beat it out of there.

If you know he has a second/vacation home, ask to join

him on a visit there. His repeated excuses for why you can't come could be a tip-off.

Look at the kind of car he drives. A minivan is almost certainly evidence that he's hitched and has a brood to squire around — unless it's loaded with work supplies.

Bottom line: it's perfectly fine and reasonable of you to be as nosy as you need to be, in order to determine whether the man you're interested in is, in fact, someone else's husband. Should he object to your nosiness, tell him to grow up — and suspect that his protests are hiding something.

7. Choose wisely. Know what you want and wait until you find it. "A sadder but wiser girl" is the poetic term that now describes you. Cheer up; it's not so terrible having a close acquaintance with the real ways of the world. For one thing, you're in a position to discern reality from fantasy, hope from hopelessness, and truth from fiction. You now know better what you yourself are about; what makes you tick and what doesn't. You're probably also less eager to waste time with people who don't serve you well. Which is why, when sticking your toe back in the ocean of romance, you should have a map of yourself — which you can draw yourself.

Get out a sheet of paper and a pen, and on the left side of the page write down everything you like — whether it's something to do (say, reading and horseback riding) or something about people (say, honesty and a sense of humor). On the right side of the page list dislikes. You may find it easier to get going by focusing first on your ex — what you liked and didn't like about him, and what you liked doing and not doing with him.

Compiling this list could take an hour or it could take days. You may, in fact, want to keep this as an ongoing exercise, expanding and even contracting the list as you think and ponder.

With this list, you now have a reference point for your manhunt. I am certainly not suggesting that the men you pursue have to match up completely with your likes and be entirely free of your dislikes. But it can't hurt a bit to have these guidelines and parameters in hand, in order to give you a reality check every now and then. That way, after you get to know the potential Mr. Right a little, you can size him up against your checklist and evaluate him accordingly.

No doubt, if the sex is great, you'll be more likely to look at all his failures to conform to your list as unimportant. But don't be fooled. Sex is always a lot better at the beginning of the relationship, when the bodies still don't know each other yet and there's that beautifully tense excitement. As time passes, sex diminishes in importance and frequency, and what you're left is…well, what you're left with. That's why what you're left with needs to be reasonably close to what you really want and need.

By the same token, don't let the flush of excitement let you talk yourself into believing you can change him into the man you want him to be. Forget it. You can no more change him than he can change you.

8. Don't rationalize or settle. I've known women

(men, too) who are so happy to actually be with someone new after getting divorced that they settle for someone like O.J. Simpson, when who they're really looking for is Cary Grant. Look, if things aren't absolutely great at the beginning, and you're having to make excuses already, don't kid yourself; it ain't getting any better than this. In fact, it's going to go downhill faster than a Himalayan avalanche.

I know why people settle — because they think that this is the only live, warm body they're going to get. But it's not true. There's always someone else.

I have a friend whose husband died unexpectedly a few years ago. At first she had a terrible time meeting someone who made her feel the way her husband did, and in her words, she "kissed a lot of frogs." Finally, she stopped trying, and for several months didn't date at all. While at lunch one day with some friends, she saw a man at the next table she considered attractive. Her friends encouraged her to be aggressive, and after a second glass of wine, she mustered the courage to introduce herself. Almost from that first moment, the sparks flew. Now, many months later, she's pretty sure that she's kissed her last frog. This guy, she insists, is a true prince.

9. Know the other person's passions and keep things interesting. The 50th wedding anniversary is considered the golden anniversary, but the golden time of any new relationship is at the beginning, when everything is fresh and new and full of excitement. Each person does whatever is possible to satisfy the other, whether that means going to plays, sporting events, book signings, flower shows, walks on the beach, candlelit picnics — anything that he or she wouldn't ordinarily do, and in fact is less likely to, as the relationship loses its newness. Normally, that's when deterioration sets in, with the partners working less hard to please the other.

Face it: relationships are hard work, "work" being the operative word. But if you can keep that in mind, and do the work that's necessary every day to try to please your partner's passions and interests, your relationship stands a much better chance of reaching full maturity instead of dying young and leaving a good-looking corpse. So make the extra effort. It will reap huge returns.

10. Communicate. Your partner cannot read your mind, nor can you read his. Which means you need to tell each other what you're thinking and feeling. But if you don't, don't complain when there's a misunderstanding.

Example: As I write, a good friend of mine is having trouble with his girlfriend. She's angry at him for "never taking me anywhere." To which he said, "But all you need to do is ask." To which she said, "Well, I keep giving you hints."

Hints are not enough. Frankly, I don't know what the big deal is about asking for exactly what you want. You wouldn't think of sitting down in a restaurant and expecting the waiter, without being told what you want, to bring you spaghetti and meatballs; nor would you have the right to get mad when fried chicken shows up on your plate. So why would you do or expect differently with your mate? Apparently, some people feel that getting what they want from their mates isn't legitimate if they actually have to ask. But that's just silly.

In my experience, open and honest communication makes most problems go away. Unfortunately, the problem with eliminating the problems is that men, by nature, aren't terrific communicators. Most of us beyond a certain age were raised to "act like a man" — that is, with a stiff upper lip. My advice, therefore, is to pick and choose the correct time and place to communicate with him. I remember during one of my marriages how I'd get up at five, work all day, eat a quick dinner at home, do some more work, and hit the sack about midnight — which was when my wife would want to get into a lengthy discussion about our relationship. It was a gargantuan miscalculation, guaranteed to make me wonder why I was even in a relationship with someone so brain-dead. We'd usually end up in a fight, which would play on my mind all night and exacerbate my exhaustion the next day...when I'd have to get up and do the whole thing all over again.

At some point we'd finally clear the air, but not before running down a list of recriminations that delayed resolution. This was as much my fault as hers. As I learned the hard way, it's hard to have a productive conversation that begins with a personal attack and is marked throughout by personal defensiveness. If you break it down to its essentials, such a conversation sounds like "You did such and such!" "I did not."

Better to talk about how you *feel* rather than what he did, because no one can argue with your feelings. Imagine if my friend's girlfriend had said to my friend, "Gil, I *feel* like you never take me anywhere," instead of "You never take me anywhere." Though only a few words apart, they're actually separated by continents in meaning. One is an attack; the other initiates conversation and may even get her what she wants. Men may not be good communicators, but they are built to solve problems — to be the knight in shining armor. Confronted by an "I feel" problem, they're likely to respond with flowers and wine; whereas if they're attacked by a "you did this and that to me," they're likely to circle the emotional wagons and pull out the big guns.

Bottom line: You can either get what you want by ordering off the menu, or you can pout about being right and misunderstood.

11. Pre-nuptials, the pros and cons. A "Pre-nup" is a very delicate subject. It's hard enough talking about the division of assets when the relationship is already crumbling; it's that much harder when you're actually talking about spending the rest of your lives together. True, it is easier in some ways to have this conversation if both of you have been married before, because you already know that "always" may not necessarily be "forever" (as Judith Krantz once pointed out). Then, too, if neither of you has substantial material assets and expect not to inherit any, the conversation goes a lot easier — in part because it's more or less an academic exercise.

For others, though, there are no easy answers. If one of you considers it appropriate to have a pre-nuptial agreement, you're pretty much stuck with resolving the issue before the wedding takes places. I know for a fact that pre-nups have derailed more bridal trains off the church aisle than have wild bachelor parties. Once the Pandora's box is opened, you have to find what seems to be a fair and equitable way through to the other side. Sometimes the negotiations themselves are a clue as to what can be expected from the marriage.

Example: I have a female friend who was broke with two young children when she met a wealthy man who stood to inherit a great deal more when his parents died. Naturally, he insisted on a pre-nup, but offered her only five grand if they divorced during the first five years, and ten grand if they divorced afterward. Against my advice, she signed the agreement, believing that she had no alternative. While I doubt the contract would hold up in court if they ever divorced, given how ridiculously low the amounts are vis-à-vis his assets, there is something to be said for a man who would lowball his wife-to-be like that — and what it says isn't good about his character. How could she possibly believe that he would be the man of her dreams when he tried to stick to her that way?

Last word on this: Always have your own attorney review your pre-nup before signing, both for legality and reasonableness, particularly if one of you is bringing a substantial fortune to the relationship.

12. Look for the little things. As a corollary to what I said above about the early days of a relationship being the golden days, keep uppermost in your mind that if your new man doesn't do all the little things he can for you while in the courting phase of your relationship, he's probably going to be a cretin after you get married.

Look, here he is, trying to put on the best show possible, and he can't be bothered helping you on with your coat, opening the door for you, walking on the curbside of a sidewalk, holding your hand, demonstrating subtle signs of affection — the little things that elevate a relationship into a love affair. What's going to happen later, when he starts losing that passion? That's what you should be asking yourself and, if necessary, answering properly. His lack of courtesies is a signal you should be paying attention to, because the little things count, and you ignore them only at your own peril down the line.

13. Know when to stop. If you have to refer to your ex-husbands by number, or sometimes forget which of them was responsible for which offenses against you, then it's time to stop looking for a new husband. You may, in fact, not be the marrying type — insofar as the vow of "till death do us part" generally indicates.

I have a friend who recently married for the sixth time, and already she's not happy with him. The woman, obviously, has issues that have nothing to do with the men she marries, and at some point she's going to have to admit that. Now, this doesn't mean she has to be alone for the rest of her life, or that she can't enjoy meaningful relationships. It just means she shouldn't be married.

I think I fall into that category, too. Something happens to me when I feel the constraint of a wedding band — not unlike, I suppose, the pet skunk I used to own. That's right, a pet skunk. He was fixed, of course, so no one could get skunked, which meant he'd waddle around the house like he was a duck (better personality, though, and no early morning quacking). Anyway, what's pertinent here is that whenever I put him in his cage, he'd throw a hissy fit, trying to get out. But if I left his cage door open, he'd often go in there to nap. Apparently, as long as he knew he had free will to come and go, he was perfectly satisfied to be wherever he was. But when his options were closed, he rebelled.

Me, I've been perfectly faithful to the woman I love for years now, and I have no desire to be with anyone else but her. Yes, some of that has to do with the normal maturation process, but some of it is knowing that my cage door is open and that I can come and go whenever I please. Rightly or wrongly, I'm not the marrying type. Lots of men are like that. Women, too. So before you think of marrying again, search your soul for the truth about which camp you fall into.

14. Know how to put fun into the relationship.
Some people feel too old to have fun. Nonsense. People start feeling old when they start acting old — that is, when they stop

having fun. At heart, we're all really still children. A miserable child is one who has no fun. So it's the same with adults. Trust me, no relationship can survive if one of the partners is miserable.

To have a good relationship, learn what makes your partner laugh — and make each other laugh every day. Maybe it's the peculiar way you do something that your partner gets a kick out of. Maybe it's the way you say something. Or maybe it's the memory of something stupid or silly you guys did together a year ago. Whatever it is on any given day that makes you laugh, that's what you pull out of the hat. Sometimes I'll put a salad bowl on my head and chase her around the room with a spoon. Sometimes I'll hike my shorts to the middle of my chest and do my "vacation dance" (don't ask). You get the point, which is that, regardless of how silly it is, I'll do what it takes to bring a smile to my lady's face. Just as she does for me, in her own inimitable way, making me sometimes gasp for breath. I'm sure it's one of the things that are keeping us both young — and interested in each other.

15. Share financial and future goals and aspirations.

You can't underestimate the importance of dreams and goals; they're what make us look forward to the future and enable us to weather rough patches in the present.

But as we age, dreams and goals change. I know mine have. For instance, when I was a boy, I wanted to grow up to be "rich and successful" — and to do that I knew I was willing to devote whatever it took to get there; if I had to sacrifice everything else in my life, well, that was the price to be paid.

But now, being older, my goals have changed. The bald accumulation of money and things is now less important to me than spending time with family and friends, and doing the activities that give me enjoyment.

While the details of your own changes may be somewhat different, I bet that you yourself have changed considerably over the years. Which is why you have to communicate constantly with your partner. You see, you don't suddenly wake up different one morning. It's a slow, ongoing process that happens a little every day. You have to know whether your goals are changing and his aren't, or vice versa, because if that's what's happening, you're in for some major disconnect down the line. And it won't be pretty.

I remember when I was working around the clock to provide my young family with a big house, nice cars, great vacations, and private schools — in short, the good life. Well, at some point my wife's goals changed and, as I pointed out earlier, she wanted me to be home every night to spend quality time with everyone. But she couldn't have it both ways — the good life and me too. And by the time we figured out what was going on, it was too late. Had we been communicating all along the way, the vast chasm might've been closed.

16. See the person for what he is, not for what you think you can make him. It's a cliché, I know, but I've rarely seen a man who starts out a relationship thinking ahead to how he can change the woman he's falling in love with, while I've rarely met a woman who hasn't begun plotting to change her man the minute they're considered an item.

Ladies, believe me, it's better to confine your fixer-upper inclinations to houses, gardens, and cars. The older the man, the more set in his ways he is. Which means that you have as much chance of changing him into the man you want him to be as you have of flying by flapping your arms hard enough. Then, too, I'm pretty sure that if you really did succeed, you wouldn't for long be happy with your new man, version 2.0. You'd want updates sooner or later. Better you should go into the relationship with the attitude that you like the guy for who he is, and accept him or not just that way.

Don't do what a friend of mine did: she married a man who she knew when they dated was a neat freak, and that this aspect of his personality was bound to drive her crazy eventually. Now, years on, it's the only thing they ever fight about, and she's ready to leave him over it. When she came to me for advice, I told her it was too late to be thinking such thoughts now. "What do you mean?" she asked. I said, "You knew what you were getting into when you married him." "Well," she said, "I thought he would change with time. But it's gotten worse."

Bottom line: Men are not blocks of clay to be molded to your artistic vision. If you really feel the need, take sculpting lessons instead.

17. Don't be afraid to back out if it's not working.

It's easy to know that you should leave a bad relationship. It's a lot harder to muster the courage to actually walk out the door.

An acquaintance of mine is on her second marriage, as is her husband. They've been together for 15 years now, probably ten of which have been miserable. They fight constantly and drink heavily, and when they're apart, each complains bitterly about the other. Both know that they should've separated long ago, but neither wants to be considered a two-time loser. Does that make sense on any level? No. Relationships that make you miserable should be starved, not fed.

The same holds true for dating. If the relationship isn't working before you put the rings on each other's fingers, it's not going to work any better after you say "I do."

Bad relationships are like bad financial investments. Once you realize that they're losers, you have to cut your losses and move on. Just as you don't throw good money after bad, don't throw good time after bad.

18. Meet the family and friends before the relationship gets going.

Apples don't fall far from their trees. And for the most part, neither do people; you can judge their fruit by the tree they came from — their families.

Want to learn things about your potential mate's personality and character that even he doesn't know? Spend some time with his family and friends. It'll tell you about his past, his present, even his future. And, if he doesn't have any friends to hang with? That right there should tell you something.

As for his family, not everyone lives near family, so it may be difficult to study them until your relationship advances far enough to safely suggest a pilgrimage. Then, too, not everyone gets along with his family, so even if your potential mate lives within quick family-visiting distance, you may not get a chance to meet them. It's important to find out why they're not on good terms, because the reasons will say as much about him as they do about his family.

When you do meet his family, you'll have some decisions to make — especially if you discover, for example, that they have more cars in their front yard than a service station and the house itself is on wheels. Now, that may be fine if you're a trailer park kind of person yourself, but if you see backgrounds, values, and interests that aren't, well, complementary to your own, you have some hard decisions to make. Like it or not, you can take the boy out of the trailer (or mansion or statehouse or whatever), but for the most part you can't take the trailer out of the boy.

19. Conduct a credit and background check. If I'd written this book even just ten years ago, I wouldn't have suggested anything of the sort. Just the cost alone would've made it prohibitive. These days, though, you can find out nearly anything you want and need to know about someone on the Internet.

So what do you want and need to know?

That question is probably best answered with a story

told to me by a woman I met in the faith-based support group I mentioned earlier. When this perfectly delightful lady met her husband, she explained, he couldn't do enough for her. But after they got married, things turned a little weird, to say the least. After paying off thousands of dollars worth of his past-due bills, spending her entire savings in the process, she found out that he was still married to his first wife. Worse, she ended up responsible for all of his new debts when he left the country to be with his family back in South America.

Another story: A close friend married a man after dating him for only a few months. This was her third marriage and his second, and at the beginning it felt wonderful enough to believe that it would be the last for both of them. The man lived in a large house, had a nice boat, drove a fancy car, and had given her a huge engagement ring. Then, a few months after the I-do's, they started having some pretty ugly arguments…about money. Turns out he'd filed for personal bankruptcy a year before they'd met, and in fact had no assets. This was a rental house, a borrowed boat, leased car — and zirconium ring. Her real jewelry he'd been stealing and pawning to pay bills.

So what's the moral? As materialistic, cynical, and unromantic as it sounds, conducting a background check on your new love can save you from letting someone ruin your life who's more cynical, materialistic, and unromantic than you could ever imagine.

Bottom line: Make sure the right guy isn't the wrong man.

20. Don't smother him. Thanks to tens of thousands of years of genetics, men (the vast majority of them, anyway) prefer to be hunters, not the hunted; to be pursuers, not the pursued. (Insert your favorite male-chauvinist-pig joke here, and laugh about the jerk with the unbuttoned shirt and gold chains who winked and said, "Hiya, gorgeous, what are you doin' the rest of my life?")

Men actually like chasing women who don't seem particularly interested in them, and in general some men prefer women who say they'd rather slit their own throats than play tonsil hockey with them. All of which is to say that men tend to lose interest in a woman who takes the fun out of the game — fun in this case being the conquest itself. If it's too easy, they're not interested.

Women, on the other hand, especially those who were married for a long time and have now been single for what seems like a long time, sometimes try too hard when they find someone they're interested in. They all but throw themselves at the new guy, which is what a friend of mine has done with her new boyfriend. Though she never smothered her first husband, she realizes that that's exactly what she's doing with her new boyfriend; "I'm just so possessive," she says. "It's like I can't help myself."

Of course, her anxiety over losing this guy too is likely to create a self-fulfilling prophecy — and even she knows that. My advice to her was to see a professional who can help her resolve her neediness, which is born out of fear of abandonment again, and to come clean with her guy about what she's feeling.

I also told her to arrange a secret sign with him, so that he can let her know quickly and cleanly when she's starting to put the figurative pillow over his face; that way, she can pull back. "If you do it right," I said, "this might become something you can build on — and get a lot of laughs out of."

Anyway, this rush to marriage, or whatever you'd prefer to call it, is an idea that should be reexamined, particularly if the couple is somewhat older. "Where is this relationship going?" may not have to be asked at all. What you may want to strive for is a relationship that is its own reward, one that offers comfort and satisfaction in the moment, and lets you sleep at night feeling eager to wake the next day. If you have that, who cares where it's going or what you call it? The journey is the destination!

21. Be careful what you wish for. In polls of women who're asked what they're looking for in a mate, the top answer is usually "sense of humor," followed by something like "decency." Down in third or fourth place is "financially independent." But you know what? Decent men with great senses of humor have been complaining for years that their empty pockets speak a lot louder to women than their personality; so really, financial independence should be number one on that list.

There's no shame in that. Just as men have been genetically programmed to hunt, women's genes tell them to nest (even when they're not true nesters). They're naturally attracted to powerful, wealthy men, someone who can keep them safe (in this case, from poverty). Unfortunately, as women sometimes learn, many men with great wealth and power often suffer from less desirable male traits. Apparently, they come in a package deal; men capable of accumulating wealth and power have the kind of testosterone that also drives them to cheat on their girlfriends and spouses.

In my view, there are five fundamental reasons why successful men may not, in fact, make the best partners — no matter how big their yachts are:

Entitlement: Men in positions of power — be it political or corporate — appear to believe that they're entitled to have a woman on the side. It's almost a cultural thing, a deserved perk that goes along with having achieved prominence. Nearly everyone in their peer group cheats, and few expect ever to get caught or be made to suffer consequences. Just as the Enron executives paid themselves huge bonuses even as the company was spiraling into bankruptcy, so too do powerful men feel entitled to take what they want — whether it's money or women — without conscience.

Risk: By nature, powerful men are risk takers. They get a drug-like high when taking risks, and the danger of getting caught is part of the game. I feel certain that what drove President Clinton to send a young intern to her knees in the Oval Office was the risk, the danger, the excitement.

Babe Magnet: It's a primal thing, this phenomenon of

women being drawn to men with power. How many unattractive men have you seen with gorgeous women on their arms? (Henry Kissinger and Jill St. John come immediately to mind.) Or how about the very old and powerful with young attractive women? (Ninety-something millionaire Pierce Marshall with twenty-something Anna Nicole Smith, for instance. Or Hugh Hefner and any of his so-called girlfriends.) If these guys drove taxis or installed drywall for a living, there's no question they wouldn't be accompanied by head-turners. Recently, a friend of mine died. He was 72 and the retired chairman of a major movie-production company. One day we were sitting around his pool, talking about whether his girlfriend, a 22-year-old stunner, was with him because of his power and money or because of love. Then she joined us and, while sitting on his lap, he asked her the question directly. "Oh, of course I'd still love you if you lost everything tomorrow," she said. "I'd miss you, but I'd still love you." The young woman's honesty was appreciated, and it points up the fact that rich and powerful men, who are already risk takers that feel entitled to get what they want, have that many more opportunities to cheat thrown at them.

Confidentiality: In the world of power, extramarital affairs are viewed as normal and ordinary. So not only do colleagues abide by the Mafia code of *omerta* — absolute silence — but so do secretaries, even without being asked to lie. In fact, I remember when one of my secretaries became close friends with my wife; she never broke the confidence. All of which means that you shouldn't expect to hear the truth from anyone in your potential mate's intimate orbit.

Unemotional: Perhaps most of all, the characteristic that might make you leery of powerful men is their ability to compartmentalize the various aspects of their lives. Example: A man can have sex with a woman without feeling any emotional attachment — and also without feeling that he's either violated a vow to you or has harmed his family. In fact, he's likely to consider himself an outstanding family man, because he provides his wife and children with what he believes his wife values most of all — money, things, and opportunities (as indeed she might).

Knowing that these are indeed the five characteristics common to most powerful men, you might want to be a little more careful of what you wish for, if what you wish for is a financially independent male.

Chapter 12

FUNDAMENTALS OF A GOOD RELATIONSHIP

As unimportant or trivial as it might seem, you really ought to analyze what went wrong the last time you walked down the aisle, and before you do it again. It's all too easy to get swept off your feet by someone who treats you well, especially if you were treated badly before. You may, in fact, be so grateful for the attention that you see and feel things that aren't really there. But if you want your next time to be better than your last time, try to make sure that the following are really there:

FRIENDSHIP. True friendship may be the most important component of a successful relationship. A few chapters ago we discussed how comfortable you felt when you were with your friends, because you share common interests and a bond of truth. Well, that's what you should be shooting for in your marital/romantic relationships, too. When you talk to older couples that have been together for decades, they'll usually attribute the relationship's longevity to the fact that they consider each other their best friend. What they've learned, and what you should know in advance, is that passion eventually wanes, and if you don't have a solid friendship to fall back on — well, it's not going to be a soft landing.

SENSE OF HUMOR: Laughing is a wonderful thing. Laughing together with someone is even better. To me, it's the ultimate foreplay.

RESPECT: Funny thing about respect — you tend to notice its absence more than its presence. You know what I mean. Someone who's condescending, demeaning, or cruel stands out a lot more than someone who's polite and courteous.

My own rule of thumb is to judge people's character by how they treat people who have less power than they do. So for an invisible test, I always observe how they treat waiters and busboys. Try it yourself; it works. If your potential mate is rude, discourteous, or nasty to such people, it's a good bet he'll eventually turn on you that way, too, no matter how well he treats you now.

INTELLECTUAL COMPATIBILITY: I was among the tens of millions who were fascinated by "Joe Millionaire" on television. As you may remember, the setup was that a Joe Sixpack kind of guy — but a stud in terms of looks — pretended to be a millionaire. Not in on the ruse were a bunch of women competing for his hand in marriage. Each of them was at first wild about him — his physique, his wallet, his eyes, his wallet, his height, his wallet, etc.

What I noticed, though, was the guy's obvious lack of intelligence. He was the equivalent of a dumb blond, which is of course appropriate, because just as the stereotypical guy doesn't care whether the beautiful blond can calculate pi to a dozen places, these women cared more about his (presumed) net worth than they did his I.Q. For a while, anyway.

As the series progressed week by week, I noticed that the women chasing him were significantly smarter and more interesting than he was, and I kept waiting to see when some of these women would get so turned off by his dim wits that they'd choose to turn their backs on what they believed was his vast fortune. One by one, the realization light bulb went on over their heads; you could see it if you watched closely enough.

Moral: If, as you rebound from divorce, you end up with some guy who's just eye candy, don't take it to the next level. Enjoy whatever he can provide you in the way of physical and ego comfort, and then move on quickly to someone who can walk and think at the same time. The connection between your minds will last long after the physical attraction between you cools off.

NO PROCRASTINATION: For years my dad would call and ask me to take off work for a few days and go fishing with him. Besides the fact that I didn't particularly like to fish, I just didn't have the time. Well, I guess I didn't want to make the time. It just wasn't a high priority for me.

Over the years, my repeatedly telling Dad that I'd let him know when we could go fishing became an ongoing family joke. Finally, on his 70th birthday in 1998, I called to say that I was at last able to go fishing with him, and we set the date — July 4th weekend, which was about five months away. Dad was so excited, he told everyone in town that his son, the big shot business executive, was taking him to a world-class fishing resort. Two months later, though, he unexpectedly and suddenly died.

I can never right this inexcusable act of procrastination, except insofar as I learned to stop — and warn others about — procrastinating. No, not every such delay is so grave, but it's absolutely true that you never really know what tomorrow holds. So make sure that you and your partner share small moments and big; that you walk on the beach together and appreciate the sunset; that you take the romantic cruise you've been talking about; that you don't put off till tomorrow what should be done today, because tomorrow may never come.

GIVE TO GET: The line's not as corny in song as it looks on the page, but that doesn't make it any less profound: "The love you take," the Beatles sang, "is equal to the love you make."

Likewise, to earn respect you've got to give respect. To earn courtesy you've got to give courtesy.

I know a man who took every opportunity to insult his wife, making backhanded comments about her and complaining constantly about her to others. Yet he couldn't understand why she sassed him when he asked her something. He didn't see that she was simply reflecting back to him how he was treating her. It's clear to me that she would've changed her attitude if he had, and I have to think that he would too eventually if she did. After all, if it's true that you give what you get, it must also be true that you get what you give. Someone has to change first.

THE GOLDEN RULE LIE: You know the words: "Do unto others as you'd have them do unto you." The golden rule is probably the first law taught to kids, as soon as they're old enough to reason even a little.

Once upon a time I sat through a business conference at which the guest speaker espoused "Golden Rule Management"; to become a successful leader and manager, he said, you have to treat people the way you want to be managed and treated.

After about three hours, I couldn't take it anymore. I raised my hand and said, "Isn't it presumptuous to assume that everyone wants to be managed or treated the way I want to be managed or treated? Frankly, it sounds to me like sheer laziness." I went on to say that truly successful, well-respected leaders take the time to find out how each person wants to be treated, and he adjusts his management style accordingly, thus maximizing the benefits of the relationship.

In many ways, the golden rule is a fallacy, both as it relates to business and interpersonally. Not everyone responds to the same stimulus, as all good sports coaches and managers learn.

Bottom line: A good relationship is based on finding out how your spouse/lover wants to be treated, and treating him that way; same with the way you want to be treated. After all, if every one of us responded similarly to the same stimuli, we'd cease to be individuals and become utterly interchangeable. And no one, I think, wants that.

KEEP THINGS IN PERSPECTIVE: As I noted earlier, things are never as good or as bad as they seem at any particular moment. Caught in a rush of emotion, both positive and negative, we tend to exaggerate the consequences and intensity of what we're feeling. So, when we're surfing a wave of euphoria, we're not likely to notice the sharks on all sides. And when we're drowning in problems, we probably won't pay attention to the buoys all around that are, in fact, opportunities and solutions.

My rule of thumb is that, unless it's a life-or-death situation, everything else has to be considered just a chance to build character.

Bottom line: In a relationship, you have to remember two simple rules. The first is that you shouldn't sweat the small stuff. And the second is that it's all small stuff.

HONESTY AND INTEGRITY: Speaking of character...

Honesty is essential to any significant relationship. Without it, there can be no trust between partners. And without trust, there can't be a partnership.

In my experience, honesty and integrity aren't hot and cold running attributes. A person is either honest, and full of integrity, or he isn't. Therefore, if you catch your man lying, cheating, and stealing from others, you have to accept that he's likely to do the same to you.

What I learned from my grandfather, a man who'd come to this country with just a few dollars and the shirt on his back, was that you could lose everything you'd worked hard to earn but still be successful if you maintained your integrity; that, he said, was something that can't be taken from you, it can only be given away.

What I learned myself was that character means doing the right thing even when no one would know the difference. Example: a friend of mine who writes speeches and stage presentations for executives of major corporations once received three checks of $20,000 each, for a total of $60,000, from one of the companies he'd worked for. In fact, he was due only $20,000, which was the amount on his invoice. On the day the three checks arrived, he called the accounts payable department and told the young man who answered about the overpayments. The young man groaned and transferred him to someone else, who transferred him to someone else, and so on, until he finally spoke with the department's supervisor, who impatiently explained to him that it would be better for everyone if he just kept the extra $40,000, given the fact that the payments had for some reason gone in separately and been approved separately; no one, she promised, would ever be wiser, while having to explain the overpayments and rebalance the accounts would be a tremendous headache. My friend hung up the phone and immediately called the chairman of the company, for whom he'd just written the speech. He related the experience and told him that he was returning, by FedEx, the extra two checks directly to him.

Honesty, integrity, and ethics are the foundation of every important relationship. They're not items to be selected or chosen at will, or switched on and off in different situations. As Teddy Roosevelt said, after firing one of his own ranch hands who'd thought he was doing a good thing by appropriating another man's steer for Roosevelt, "A man who would steal *for* me would also steal *from* me."

Bottom line: Make sure your partner has the qualities that build trust. Without them, you'll have no foundation at all.

UNCONDITIONAL LOVE: You're a Mafia hit man. You come home from a long hard day of whacking guys, breaking some knee caps, and lying to federal prosecutors — and there, wagging his tail, excited to see you when you step through the door, is your beloved Yellow Lab. He doesn't care that you're going to burn in hell. He just loves you for who you are.

Baby, that's unconditional love.

And it's what you should strive for in your new relationship.

Unconditional love is being excited to see you, no matter where or when. It's missing you when you're apart, even if you've just gone to the market and back. It's thinking about what will please you, even when you haven't asked. It's knowing that, regardless of how well or badly things are going, you have a special place in his heart.

But unconditional love can get tricky when it's translated from male to female. Men view love differently than women do. More specifically, they view "being in love" differently than just "loving." To a woman, "in love" means fireworks, passion, euphoria. To a man, "in love" is reserved for the woman he wants to marry. Most men don't understand that a woman can love someone and marry him; they don't know that women don't have to be "in love" to say I do.

So please, make sure you define your terms with each other, so that you're both speaking the same language — but most of all because you want to know that his love for you really is unconditional.

In sum, it's absolutely critical that you share with your new/potential mate some common perspective on each of the above concepts or attributes. If you don't, it's going to be a short, and probably very unhappy, relationship.

EPILOGUE

CLOSING THOUGHTS

I sincerely hope that you've enjoyed reading this book as much as I've enjoying writing it. I admit to having had moments of trepidation, thanks to breaking the male code of silence on several subjects. But as I said earlier, if this book helps to save one marriage or relationship, or eases one person's journey from divorce to health, I'll consider the project an enormous success. By the way, to confirm that I was on the right path, I let two male friends of mine read the first manuscript draft. The one that was going through a fairly ugly divorce said "Holy crap!" (Cleaned up version). "What the hell are you trying to do? I better get my divorce over with before this book comes out!" I think I received the validation I was looking for.

Before going, let me share a couple of final thoughts. The most important, I'd say, is that you shouldn't show this book to your husband or boyfriend, or tell him anything you'd read. You absolutely do not want to give him any ideas. If he's not creative enough to come up with his own ways to lie, cheat, and steal, don't help him.

The last thought I'd like to share with you came from the daughter of a friend of mine, a young woman whose brain I was picking about relationships, marriage, and divorce. She summed up everything in a quotation from William Jennings Bryan, the great American politician and orator. "Destiny," he said, "is not a matter of chance; it's a matter of choice. It's not a thing to be waited for; it's a thing to be achieved."

So there it is, then. We choose whether or not to achieve life and love. And while we're making our choices, it's wise to keep in mind that the road to happiness is always under construction.

QUOTES FROM COUPLES
MARRIED
OVER **30** YEARS

"If he helps around the house – washes the dishes, cooks, vacuums – and it's not quite up to your standards, don't complain. Be happy he is making an effort to help."
— *Married 45 years*

"Respect and a sense of humor are key. The sense of humor needs to kick in when the respect is temporarily wavering"
— *Married 35 years*

"Accept that you can't change someone. You have to learn to live with whatever annoys you, and remember that you have as many faults as your spouse does."
— Married 40 years

"You have to be best friends, have mutual respect, trust, and be truly comfortable, not the pursuit of personal dreams."
— Married 30 years

"When she gets mad, I just shut up, and she gets tired of talking. After a while, it's over. In all our years being together, we have never had an argument!"
— Married 56 years

"Love each other, of course. You also need trust, patience, and lots and lots of compromise."
— Married 41 years

"You have to respect the other person, and keep a sweet mouth. That is, always have something nice to say."

— *Married 55 years*

"Our secret to a long marriage? Hiring a good cleaning person"

— *Married 30 years*

"If your spouse asks you to do something, just do it, right then. It's easier to do that than it is to argue over it."

— *Married 40 years*

"Always be grateful to your spouse. And say so, often."

— *Married 30 years*

"Don't expect the lust to carry you through. It doesn't last, but friendship does."
— *Married 40 years*

"We've always put each other first. If you don't do that, especially with children in the picture, you're lost. Your top priority is him, and his top priority is you. If you get that right, everything else will be fine—your children will be fine, your home will run well, and you'll both feel loved and important."
— *Married 40 years*

About the Author

Will Willis was born and raised in Newport, Rhode Island. He attended Columbia College and Columbia Business School, earning a BA and MBA. For most of his adult life, he headed companies that make and market many of America's most recognized consumer products, including Playtex, Cheetos, and Mennen. Will currently lives in Florida with Jean and her daughter Alexis, who are the beneficiaries of all the wisdom he gleaned from his two marriages and two divorces. Nowadays, family time is spent on the boat, or motorcycling, or walking his two yellow Labs. Will's first book was "If You're Not Living On The Edge, You're Taking Up Too Much Space" – a comprehensive guide for aspiring business people in need of career management guidance.

NOTES